The Global Business Revolution and the Cascade Effect

The Global Business Revolution and the Cascade Effect

Systems Integration in the Global Aerospace, Beverage and Retail Industries

Peter Nolan, Jin Zhang and Chunhang Liu

First published 2007 by
PALGRAVE MACMILLAN
Houndmills, Basingstoke, Hampshire RG21 6XS and
175 Fifth Avenue, New York, N.Y. 10010
Companies and representatives throughout the world

PALGRAVE MACMILLAN is the global academic imprint of the Palgrave Macmillan division of St. Martin's Press, LLC and of Palgrave Macmillan Ltd. Macmillan® is a registered trademark in the United States, United Kingdom and other countries. Palgrave is a registered trademark in the European Union and other countries.

ISBN-13: 978–0–230–01358–2 hardback
ISBN-10: 0–230–01358–9 hardback

This book is printed on paper suitable for recycling and made from fully managed and sustained forest sources. Logging, pulping and manufacturing processes are expected to conform to the environmental regulations of the country of origin.

A catalogue record for this book is available from the British Library.

Library of Congress Cataloging-in-Publication Data
Nolan, Peter, 1949–
    The global business revolution and the cascade effect : systems
    integration in the global aerospace, beverage and retail industries /
    Peter Nolan, Jin Zhang, Chunhang Liu.
        p.   cm.
    Includes bibliographical references and index.
    ISBN-13: 978–0–230–01358–2 (cloth)
    ISBN-10: 0–230–01358–9 (cloth)
    1. Industrial organization (Economic theory)   2. Industrial
    concentration.   I. Zhang, Jin, 1967–   II. Liu, Chunhang.   III. Title.
    HD2326.N65 2007
    338.8—dc22   2006051449

10   9   8   7   6   5   4   3   2   1
16   15   14   13   12   11   10   09   08   07

Contents

List of Tables and Figures

Tables

Figures

Acronyms and Abbreviations

ACI	Australian Consolidated Industries (Australian glass manufacturer)
AIG	American International Group
AXA	French insurance company
BOC	The BOC Group plc (formerly known as British Oxygen Company)
BP	BP plc (formerly known as British Petroleum plc)
BSN	BSN Glasspack SA.
BTR	BTR plc (its packaging business was acquired by O-I in 1998)
CCE	Coca-Cola Enterprises
CHF	Swiss francs
COFCO	China National Cereals, Oils & Foodstuffs Corporation
CSD(s)	Carbonated soft drink(s)
CSFB	Crédit Suisse First Boston
DAF	DAF Trucks NV (Netherlands truck manufacturer)
DTI	Department of Trade and Industry
EBITDA	Earnings before interest, taxation, depreciation and amortization
EU	European Union
FDI	Foreign direct investment
FMCG	Fast moving consumer goods
FT	*Financial Times*
GDP	Gross domestic product
GE	General Electric Company
GKN	Guest Keen & Nettlefolds
GM	brand name for General Motors Corporation
GNP	Gross national product
GSK	GlaxoSmithKline
IBM	IBM Corporation (formerly known as International Business Machines Corporation)
ICI	Imperial Chemical Industries plc
IHT	*International Herald Tribune*
IISI	International Iron and Steel Institute
IISS	International Institute for Strategic Studies
IMRA	International Mass Retail Association
ISP(s)	Internet service provider(s)

IT	Information technology
JV	Joint venture
KHS	Filling machinery company
KKR	Kohlberg Kravis Roberts & Co.
M&A	Merger(s) and acquisition(s)
MNC(s)	Multinational corporation(s)
MRO	Maintenance, repair and overhaul
MSDW	Morgan Stanley Dean Witter
NDP	The NDP Group Inc (market research firm)
NTT	Nippon Telegraph & Telephone Corp (Japanese telecomms company)
OEM	Original equipment manufacturer
P&G	Procter & Gamble
PEN	Polyethylene naphthalate
PET	Polyethylene terephthalate
PPP	Purchasing power parity (dollars)
PTA	Purified terephthalic acid
R&D	Research and development
RTS	Ready to serve
SCMC	Supply and marketing company (Coca-Cola)
SCMP	*South China Morning Post*
SEN	German packaging equipment manufacturer
SIC	Standard Industrial Classification
SIG	Swiss International Group
SIPRI	Stockholm International Peace Research Institute
SKU(s)	Stock keeping unit(s)
SOE(s)	State-owned enterprise(s)
TCCC	The Coca-Cola Company
TPG	TPG Logistics (global logistics company)
UNCTAD	United Nations Conference on Trade and Development
UNDP	United Nations Development Programme
USDA	United States Department of Agriculture
UV	Ultraviolet
WAW	*Ward's Auto World*
WPP	WPP Group (global public relations company)
WTO	World Trade Organization

Introduction

Since the 1990s, the global economic environment has undergone profound changes. The liberalization of trade and capital flows, rapid advances in information technology, development of global capital markets and the trend of privatization and deregulation in many parts of the world have resulted in an explosion of merger and acquisition (M&A) activities among firms in high-income countries. After 1980, M&A activities completed worldwide grew at an average annual rate of 42 per cent to reach US\$ 2.3 trillion in 1999, or 8 per cent of world GDP. Between 1980 and 2000, M&A activities worldwide generated a combined transaction value of more than US\$ 12 trillion. The world has not seen this magnitude of business restructuring since the merger wave that created giant American corporations at the turn of the nineteenth century. The outcome of the latest wave of M&A activities is no less than a profound transformation at the heart of the global business structure. Nolan (2001a) has named this phenomenon 'the global business revolution'. The global business revolution has fundamentally changed the nature of the capitalist firm, the pattern of competition and the way in which economic production is organized in much of the global economy.

This book aims to contribute towards an understanding of the nature of the modern firm and the reality of global business structure at the dawn of the twenty-first century. Such an understanding is critical in economic policy analysis. For high-income countries, a predominant portion of economic transactions is conducted within the firm. In the United States, for example, as much as two-thirds of economic transactions in terms of value is carried out inside the firm (Wolf, 2005). For most low-income countries, powerful global firms based in high-income countries are already playing an important role in international trade, financing, procurement, service provisions or direct production in the local economies. In China, for example, multinational corporations (MNCs) have become an important force in the economy even before the WTO rules are fully implemented. Between 1990 and 2000, the share of MNCs in China's manufacturing sales rose rapidly from 2.3 per cent to 31.3 per cent. By 2001, MNCs had accounted for 50 per cent of the country's exports (44 per cent of manufacturing exports) and 9.5 per cent of its urban employment (UNCTAD, 2002: 154). At the same time, MNC-related products and services accounted for a dominant share of total sales in industries ranging from automobiles, commercial aircraft, high-technology IT hardware and software, high-end consumer products, branded food and beverages, to specific segments of the retail industry in China. In many low-income countries, it is increasingly the case that indigenous firms and economic entities are either working for or competing against global firms based in high-income countries. In the international economy, the multinational corporation is playing an increasingly important role in international trade and investment. As much as one-third of world trade at the end of the twentieth century is conducted within multinational corporations as intra-firm trade (UNCTAD, 2002: 153).

The analysis in our research follows the value chain framework. The *value chain* refers to 'the full range of activities which are required to bring a product or service from conception, through the different phases of production (involving a combination of physical transformation and the input of various producer services), delivery to final consumers, and final disposal after use' (Kaplinsky and Morris, 2000: 4). *Value chain analysis* focuses on the dynamics of inter-firm linkages during this entire process of value creation. It seeks to understand the competitive strategies and sources of competitive advantage of firms, which not only determine value creation by the collective chain but also govern the power relationships among participants within the chain. Value chain analysis recognises the dynamic power relationships between collaborating and competing firms. The value chain perspective offers a more comprehensive view of how resource allocation decisions are made not only within the firm but also in the entire value chain, that is, outside the legal boundaries of the firm itself. The traditional transaction cost theory, with its focus on the *firm versus market* dichotomy, has underestimated the complexity of economic relationships in the modern global economy. In contrast, the value chain framework generates a holistic view of how competitive advantages are constructed for the modern capitalist firm. Value chain analysis therefore tends to generate more useful insights for industrial policy in advanced economies.

For developing countries, a value chain perspective of the global economic structure is particularly important. For their firms, access to developed country markets has become increasingly dependent upon entering into the global commodity chains of core firms based in high-income countries (Humphrey and Schmitz, 2001; Gereffi, Humphrey and Sturgeon, 2001). The participation of firms from low-income countries in the global economy is therefore not just governed by trade policies but also by the strategic decisions of the core firms in the value chains. This has been a central theme in several value chain studies, including those on the textile and garment trade between East Asian countries and the United States (Bonacich *et al.*, 1994; Gereffi, 1999), the horticultural trade between Africa and the United Kingdom (Dolan and Humphrey, 2000), and the trade in footwear from China and Brazil to US and European markets (Schmitz and Knorringa, 2000). By focusing on inter-firm linkages in global value chains, value chain analysis constitutes a highly useful tool for understanding the way in which indigenous firms from low-income countries participate in the global economy.

In this book, we focus on three major aspects of the global business revolution. First, the explosion of M&A activities at the end of the twentieth century has produced unprecedented levels of concentration in almost all of the high value-added, high technology parts of the world economy. Global competition has forced firms in related industries to consolidate in order to achieve greater economies of scale and scope in critical business activities that constitute core competitive advantages of firms. These activities include branding, technology acquisition, human resources, financing, research and development (R&D), information technology (IT) and logistics.

Second, competitive pressures and increasing complexity involved in organizing economic production have strengthened the planning and coordination function of leading firms, that is, 'systems integrators' or core firms, in global value chains. While traditional theory has constrained the administrative function of the firm to intra-firm activities, our observation is that the planning and coordination function of systems integrators has extended beyond the legal boundaries of the firm to reach segments deep in the value chain.

Third, these systems integrators persistently pass on the pressure for consolidation to their first-tier suppliers, through increased require-ments in product quality, costs and technological progress. As first-tier suppliers consolidate, they pass along the same pressure to *their* suppliers through the same mechanisms. The pressure for consolidation therefore 'cascades' down the supply chain so that economies of scale and scope are maximized in key business activities of the value chain. Such is the 'cascade effect' that we have observed in many industries during the global business revolution.

We will analyse the main aspects of the global business revolution by examining three case studies: the global aerospace, beverage and retail industries. The case studies grow out of our research on the structural changes in the value chains of these industries during the global business revolution. Data for the research have been obtained from company reports and documents, industry reports, and in-depth interviews with company management, suppliers and customers in the three industries. These interviews yielded an enormous amount of insight into the evolving global industry environment, company strategy and the dynamics of inter-firm linkages in global value chains.

In this book, chapter 1 outlines the academic debate surrounding the nature of the capitalist firm and that of competition. The mainstream and non-mainstream views yield very different interpretations of the recent changes in global business structure and implications for policy. Chapter 2 examines the general outcome of the global business revolution at the end of the twentieth century, which is the unprecedented level of concentration in many industries at a global level. It introduces the concept of systems integration as a management innovation to deal with the complexities in global value chains, and the emergence of the 'external firm' and the 'cascade effect' as a result.

Chapters 3, 4 and 5 are case studies of three different industries – aerospace, beverages and retail. In aerospace, the industries' products are at the highest levels of technology and their nature is constantly changing. A single large commercial aeroplane, such as a Boeing 747–400 or 777, costs over US$ 200 million. In the beverage industry, the products have hardly changed at all over many decades. A can of Coca-Cola costs around US$ 1. The retail industry engages in the buying and selling of food products, apparel and consumer goods, connecting a wide range of consumer and agricultural industries to a vast number of individual buyers. By analysing such different industries, we hope to examine the common processes at work. The case studies will closely examine the industry dynamics at different levels of the value chain and the complex relationship between the systems integrator and other value chain participants.

Chapter 6 draws upon the implications of the global business revolution for industrial catch-up in developing countries: in other words, how has the global business revolution affected the possibilities for firms from developing countries to upgrade their capabilities and compete on the 'global level playing field'? It sheds light on the nature of the task facing firms and policy makers in developing countries in their attempt to 'catch-up' with firms from high-income countries. It suggests that because of the 'cascade effect', the challenge for developing countries is much greater than is commonly thought to be the case.

1
The Debate

An increasing amount of literature has been devoted to the recent changes in the global business structure. However, researchers have not agreed on the nature of these structural changes nor on the implications for catch-up for firms in developing countries. The differences seem to stem from a fundamental divergence in the view of the nature of capitalist competition and the nature of the firm.

1.1 The mainstream views

The 'mainstream' view of the competitive process believes that the perfectly competitive model best describes the essence of capitalist competition. Departures from it are viewed as exceptional. At the heart of the mainstream view is the self-equilibrating mechanism of market competition. It is believed that the basic driver of the capitalist process, competition, ensures that if any firm enjoys supernormal profits rivals will soon enter to bid away those profits and undermine any temporary market dominance that the incumbent enjoys. The neo-classical approach emphasizes the importance of competition among small firms as the explanation for the prosperity of the advanced economies, especially the United States. The Chicago economist George Stigler concluded that as much as 85 per cent of the US economy in the mid-twentieth century was 'competitive' (quoted in Friedman, 1962: 122). Friedman himself thought that there was 'a general bias and tendency to overemphasize the importance of the big versus the small ... As I have studied economic activities in the United States, I have become increasingly impressed with how wide is the range of problems and industries that can be treated as if it were competitive' (Friedman, 1962: 120–3).

Coase's seminal paper *The Nature of the Firm* (1937), first examined the reasons for the existence of the capitalist firm. Coase proposed that firms exist to minimize transaction costs. Since then, the modern corporation has been mainly analysed as 'the product of a series of organizational innovations that have had the purpose and effect of economizing on transaction costs' (Williamson, 1981: 1537). In recent decades, transaction cost theory has sought to explain the existence and expansion of large multinational firms as the internalization of market failures in setting prices on technology (Williamson, 1981), the 'know-how' in maintaining product quality (Casson, 1982), and knowledge in general with regards to technology development and application, quality control and branding (Rugman, 1982). In this view, inter-firm relationships are characterized by arm's-length transactions that constitute the market. Firms are therefore 'islands in a sea of market transactions' (Richardson, 1972).

In the mainstream view, it is inconceivable for any one or any few firms to grow to dominate entire sectors of the economy, since managerial diseconomies of scale set in after firms reach a certain size. In transaction cost theory, the size of the firm is determined at the boundary where the cost of organizing exchange through the market mechanism is compared with that of administrative organization within the firm. Coase (1937) argued that as firms grow, they may run into *diminishing returns to the entrepreneurial function*, as the entrepreneur fails to allocate resources to their best use in an increasingly large administrative organization. This failure then contributes to a rise in factor prices in relation to a smaller firm.

A classic, more poetic expression of the nature of competition and the limit to firm size is contained in Marshall's *Principles of Economics*, first published in 1890, in which he compared competition with a forest, with no single tree ever growing above a certain height:

[H]ere we may read a lesson from the young trees of the forest as they struggle upwards through the benumbing shade of their older rivals. Many succumb on the way, and a few only survive: those few become stronger with every year, they get a larger share of light and air with every increase of their height, and at last in their turn they tower above their neighbours, and seem as though they would grow on for ever and for ever become stronger as they grow. But they do not. One tree will last longer in full vigour and attain a greater size than another; but sooner or later age tells on them all. Though the taller ones have a better access to light and air than their rivals, they gradually lose vitality; and one after another they give place to others, which though of less material strength, have on their side the vigour of youth ... [I]n almost every trade there is a constant rise and fall of large businesses, at any one moment some firm being in the ascending phase and others in the descending (Marshall, 1920: 315–16).

Although M&A activities in recent decades have dramatically increased the size and dominance of large capitalist firms, the vast majority of mainstream economists believe that 'mergers mostly fail'.[1] A series of research found that the majority of UK and US takeovers have not improved firm performance (Meeks, 1977; Ravenscraft and Scherer, 1987; Agarwal *et al.*, 1992; Gregory, 1997). Such studies are usually based on an analysis of either short-term accounting profits or returns to shareholders. The explanation that is usually advanced for mergers is the pursuit of power and wealth by CEOs, who pursue their own selfish interests at the expense of shareholders.

In recent years, the argument has gained ground that advances in information technology have created the possibility for a radical change in the nature of the firm. Activities that were formerly rational to carry out within the firm, can now be performed by networks of small firms connected by the Internet (Castells, 2000). This is widely thought to herald the rise of a new form of 'post-Fordist' economic system based around 'clusters' of small businesses that can both compete and cooperate at different times (Piore and Sabel, 1984; Porter, 1990). This view appeared to be strongly reinforced by the rapid rise in the extent of outsourcing of activities that were formerly carried on within the firm. In Coasian terms (Coase, 1988), the very boundaries of the firm have shifted. Many researchers argued that these changes heralded a new epoch of production systems based around a greatly increased role for small and medium firms, the so-called 'meso' level of business activity, relative to large corporations. They argue that the large corporation is 'hollowing out', and rapidly becoming an 'endangered species': 'While big companies control ever larger flows of cash, they are exerting less and less direct control over business activity. They are, you might say, growing hollow' (Malone and Laubacher, 1998: 147).

In the mainstream view, the spread of markets at the regional and global levels has increased the scope of competition for firms and enlarged the number of choices for consumers in a 'free market system'. Markets have become so vast, spread across the whole world, that it is hard to imagine that any firm or small group of firms could dominate any given sector. An early version of this optimistic view of the consequences of the widening of markets for industrial concentration was given in Friedman (1962):

> the developments in transportation and communications of local regional markets and widening the scope within which competition could take place have been given much less attention. The growing concentration of the automobile industry is a commonplace; growth of the trucking industry which reduces dependence on large railroads passes with little attention; so does the declining monopoly in the steel industry (ibid.: 123).[2]

More recently, Wolf (2005) gave an optimistic, if not idealistic, view of 'the global market economy', in which 'nobody is in charge':

> Think for a moment about what our economy achieves. We can buy food produced all over the world, which is then bought, processed, distributed and sold through a long chain of wholesalers and retailers to satisfy our varying tastes. The food will be extraordinarily safe. One can buy clothing made by workers in China, India, Italy or Mexico, in a staggering number of different fabrics and styles. For personal transport, one can choose from many varieties of motor car; for entertainment, one can select a DVD player and flat-screen television; for work, leisure or personal bureaucracy, one can buy a personal computer. An army of competing inventors, designers, producers and distributors try to meet all these and many other demands . . . We take all this for granted. Yet it is extraordinary. What makes it far more extraordinary – and to many quite scary – is that nobody is in charge. Adam Smith's metaphor of the invisible hand remains as illuminating as ever (Wolf, 2005: 45).

It seems that, by joining this global 'free market' system, indigenous firms from low-income countries would have much greater opportunities for profitable growth and would eventually 'catch up' with industry leaders based in high-income countries in size and capabilities. The spread of global markets has greatly reinforced the belief that 'catch-up' at the level of the firm is the normal path of capitalist development.

Like the young trees in the forest, firms from developing countries (many of whom are entering the global market for the first time), although much smaller in size and inferior in capabilities, will eventually catch-up with their older and larger rivals (that is, established firms in high-income countries) through the process of global competition. In this view, there are limitless opportunities for capabilities enhancement and growth if firms from developing countries are forced into competition on the 'global level playing field'.

1.2   The non-mainstream views

From the earliest stages in the development of modern capitalism, there were economists who believed that capitalism contained an inherent tendency towards industrial concentration. Marx, in *Capital*, Volume 1, argued that the 'laws of centralization of capitals' or the 'attraction of capital by capital' underlined the competitive process in the capitalist system. The driving force of concentration was competition itself, which pressures firms to cheapen the cost of production by investing ever-larger amounts of capital in new means of production and in 'the technological application of science', which in turn creates barriers to entry. Benefiting from economies of scale, well-managed large firms can achieve lower factor prices, which constitute a critical competitive advantage:

> The battle of competition is fought by cheapening commodities. The cheapness of commodities depends, *ceteris paribus*, on the productiveness of labour, and this again on the scale of production. Therefore the larger capital beats the smaller . . . Everywhere the increased scale of industrial establishments is the starting-point for a more comprehensive organization of the collective work of many, for a wider development of their material motive force – in other words, for the progressive transformation of isolated processes of production, carried on by customary methods, into processes of production socially combined and scientifically arranged (Marx, 1867: 626–7).

The advantages of firm size have been continuously examined and explained in later writings. Marshall's *Principles of Economics* provides numerous reasons to explain 'the advantages that a large business of almost any kind, nearly always has over a small one' (Marshall, 1920: 282). These included economies in procurement, transport costs, marketing, branding, distribution, knowledge, human resources, and management (ibid.: 282–4). By contrast, his explanation of 'managerial diseconomies of scale' resorts merely to an analogy ('the trees in the forest') without logic or evidence.

Penrose's path-breaking book, *The Theory of the Growth of the Firm*, addresses directly the issue of possible limits to the growth of the firm. Like Marshall, she identifies several potential advantages that can be enjoyed by the large firm (Penrose, 1995: 89–92). She considers that the most significant advantages for the large firm are those that she terms 'managerial economies', which include scale advantages in administration, procurement, marketing, financing and research:

> Managerial economies are held to result when a larger firm can take advantage of an increased division of managerial labour and of the closely allied mechanization of certain administrative processes; make more intensive use of existing managerial resources by the 'spreading' of overheads; obtain economies from buying and selling on a larger scale; use reserves more economically; acquire capital on cheaper terms; and support large scale research (Penrose, 1995: 92).

Penrose concluded that there were no theoretical limits to the size of the firm: 'We have found nothing to prevent the indefinite expansion of firms as time passes, and clearly if some of the economies of size are economies of expansion, there is no reason to assume that a firm would ever reach a size in which it has taken full advantage of all these economies' (Penrose, 1995: 99). She also postulated that larger firms may also benefit from the *economies of growth*, where 'the organization and execution of an expansion on the required scale is only possible for firms already large'. She observed that while firms have been growing larger in size, they have not necessarily become less efficient; management innovations, such as the M-form organization (multi-divisional), have continuously allowed firms to avoid the diseconomies of management.

While mainstream analyses have always played down the importance of large firms, several studies show that large firms play an important role in promoting economic growth in a modern economy. Chandler (1990) has demonstrated the central role of the large, oligopolistic firm in technical progress in the business history of today's high-income countries. This was, in its turn, central to the whole growth dynamic of modern capitalism. He has shown that the modern industrial enterprise 'played a central role in creating the most technologically advanced, fastest growing industries of their day'. These industries, in turn, were 'the pace-setters of the industrial sector of their economies'. They provided an underlying dynamic in the development of modern industrial capitalism (Chandler, 1990: 593). Chandler emphasizes the paradox that even as the number of firms in a given sector shrinks, competition between increasingly powerful firms can intensify: 'market share and profits changed constantly, which kept oligopolies from becoming stagnant and monopolistic' (Chandler and Hikino, 1997: 31).

The succession of mainstream studies that purport to show the irrationality of mergers and acquisitions are almost entirely based on the analysis of the consequences for shareholder value in the short term. The much smaller number of studies that analyse the long-term impact of mergers and acquisitions on business survival and growth show a different story (Chandler, 1990; Nolan, 2001a, 2001b; Boston Consulting Group, 2004). They suggest, rather, that well-selected and well-executed mergers and acquisitions that have a clear strategic purpose, can increase the business capability of the firm concerned. They can strengthen the firm's presence in given geographical markets, increase their access to technologies they formerly did not possess, acquire scarce human resources, add valuable brands to their portfolio, and enable long-term savings through economies of scale and scope in procurement, research and development, and marketing.

Several studies have found that the spread of markets at a global level has given rise to giant multinational companies that are rapidly becoming a dominating force in modern economic life. In the early 1970s, on the eve of the modern epoch of globalization, Stephen Hymer visualized the possible outcome of the capitalist process if existing restrictions on merger and acquisition were lifted:

> Suppose giant multinational corporations (say 300 from the US and 200 from Europe and Japan) succeed in establishing themselves as the dominant form of international enterprise and come to control a significant share of industry (especially modern industry) in each country. The world economy will resemble more and more the United States economy, where each of the large corporations tends to spread over the entire continent, and to penetrate almost every nook and cranny (Hymer, 1972).

More recently, there has emerged an increasing amount of research on the power and dominance of global corporations. Anderson and Cavanagh (2000) found that of the 100 largest economies in the world at the end of the twentieth century, 51 were corporations (based on corporate sales and country GDPs). The New Global History Project, sponsored by the Toynbee Prize Foundation, has spawned a series of studies on global corporations, in the belief that we have entered a 'global epoch' of unprecedented corporate power. In *Global Inc.*, Gabel and Bruner (2003) showed that multinational corporations have been increasing almost exponentially in size and scope in the past few decades. They found that the 53 largest corporations in the world have become wealthier and larger (in terms of sales) than 120–130 nation states in 2000. While comparing corporate sales to country GDPs raises methodological questions, it does underline the immense size of multinational corporations at the end of the twentieth century.[3] Multinational corporations are generating powerful impacts on 'practically every sphere of modern life, from policy making in regard to the environment and international security; from problems of identity and community; and from the future of work to the future of the nation state' (Gabel and Bruner, 2003: vi). As the new Leviathans of our time, multinational corporations have emerged 'from the depths of humanity's creative powers' and are increasingly challenging the power of the nation states (Chandler and Mazlish, 2005: 2).

In a global market dominated by powerful firms from high-income countries, the prospects for firms from low-income countries do not seem promising. Dicken (2003) offers a summary of various studies on the global value chains of textile, automobile, semiconductor, financial services and distribution industries. The tendency towards consolidation and concentration is common in every industry under discussion. The strategies of the leading firms, most of which are based in high-income countries, have played an important role in shaping value chain structures in terms of location of production and patterns of coordination. In the end, Dicken draws upon the general implications of the un-level playing field opened up by globalization for industrial development in low-income countries:

> 'Openness', then, is the name of the game. But this will work only if the playing field is relatively level – which it clearly is not. And it also has to work both ways – which clearly it does not... In other words, the odds are stacked against [developing countries]... Simply opening up a developing economy on its own will almost certainly lead to further disaster. There is the danger of local businesses being wiped out by more efficient foreign competition before they can get a toehold in the wider world. (Dicken, 2003: 575)

1.3 Unanswered questions

As discussed, divergent views exist on the competitive process in the capitalist system and the nature of the capitalist firm. Conditions in the world economy in the 1990s formed a favourable environment for the further growth of large firms at a global level. During this period, many of the technological and institutional constraints on firm growth were removed. Vast regions of the world were opened for competition. Privatization was enacted across almost all countries. Cross-border restrictions on mergers and acquisitions were removed from all but a few sectors. The period provided a unique opportunity to test competing views of the competitive process. Have there indeed been natural limitations on the size of large firms in this favourable environment of growth? How have large firms dealt with the complexity in managing in a global economy? How have the ways in which firms organize economic production changed? How have these changes affected the structure of industries and value chains? What are the implications for firms from developing countries?

The answers to these questions are extremely important to policy making in advanced as well as developing countries. The following chapters will closely examine the key aspects of the global business revolution with respect to important changes in the nature of competition and that of the capitalist firm. They will seek to generate important insights into the reality underlying the global business environment at the beginning of the twenty-first century.

2
The Global Business Revolution, Systems Integration and the Cascade Effect

The past two decades have seen a profound change in the global business structure, driven by an explosion in M&A activities in many high value-added industries in the world economy. This chapter examines the key features of the global merger wave as well as its impact on global industry concentration. It also introduces the two other key characteristics of the global business revolution at the end of the twentieth century: the practice of *systems integration* by the core firm and the *cascade effect* in global value chains as a result of it. They have profoundly changed the way in which production is organized in the modern capitalist system.

2.1   The merger wave at the end of the twentieth century[4]

Between 1980 and 2000, M&A transactions had a combined value of more than US$ 12 trillion. During this period, the trend of global business restructuring seemed to be accelerating: between 1980 and 1999, M&As completed worldwide grew at an average annual rate of 42 per cent, to reach US$ 2.3 trillion in 1999, or 8 per cent of the world GDP (UNCTAD, 2000). The top 50 US mergers during this 20-year period alone accounted for nearly US$ 2 trillion. The largest US M&A transactions tended to focus on service industries, with M&As in financial services, media and entertainment, and telecommunication services accounting for 25 per cent, 22 per cent and 21 per cent respectively of transaction value. By 1990, one-third of the giants in America's *Fortune* 500 in 1980 had lost their independence; five years later, another 40 per cent had disappeared (*Economist*, 29 January 2000).

Cross-border M&A

Between 1980 and 2000, 25 per cent of the M&A activities involved cross-border transactions. Between 1987 and 1999, a total of 44,583 cross-border transactions took place with a total value of US$ 2.8 trillion (UNCTAD, 2000). By 2000, cross-border transactions had amounted to US$ 720 billion, or nearly one-third of all M&A transactions in the world. The trend of cross-border M&A was widespread in manufacturing and services sectors. Between 1987 and 1999, the value of cross-border M&As was evenly split between manufacturing (49 per cent) and service sectors (49 per cent) with primary sectors accounting for a minute share of 2 per cent. During this period, M&A activities shifted towards service sectors, whose share of transaction value increased from 56 per cent in 1990 to 71 per cent in 1999, while that of the manufacturing sector declined from 41 per cent to 27 per cent. Among the different sectors, the financial industry witnessed the largest share of M&A transactions, accounting for US$ 690 million in M&A value between 1987 and 1999, or 25 per cent of all cross-border transactions during this period. The surging level of M&A transactions in the finance sector reflected the widespread trend of financial deregulation and globalization of finance. Other active M&A sectors include chemicals, energy, telecommunications, transportation and logistics, food and beverages, electrical equipment, business services and metals and metal products (see Table 2.1).

Table 2.1   Distribution of cross-border M&As by value, 1987–99

	Value of transactions (US$ billion)	% of total
Service sectors	1,391	49
– Finance	690	25
– Transport, storage and communications	211	7
– Electricity, gas and water	135	5
Manufacturing sectors	1,369	49
– Chemicals	298	11
– Coke, petro and nuclear fuel	185	7
– Food, beverages and tobacco	181	6
– Electrical and electrical equipment	164	6
– Auto	107	4
– Metal and metal products	106	4
Primary sectors	56	2
Total cross-border transactions	2,816	100

Source: Compiled by author from UNCTAD (2000)

Large multinational firms based in high-income countries dominated cross-border transactions. Between 1987 and 1999, firms from developed countries accounted for 87 per cent (or US$ 2.45 trillion) of the transactions, among which firms from the European Union accounted for 40 per cent (or US$ 1.1 trillion), while American firms accounted for 35 per cent (or US$ 1.0 trillion). Mergers and acquisitions deals with size above US$ 1 billion accounted for over 66 per cent of the total cross-border transaction value in 1999. During 1987–99, the top ten multinational firms concluding the largest cross-border M&A deals accounted for 13 per cent of the total value of deals. Because of the mega deals in the later half of the 1990s, this share increased from 15 per cent during 1996–97 to 31 per cent during 1998–99.

Table 2.2 shows the top 20 multinational firms with the largest cross-border M&A activity between 1987 and 1999. One striking aspect of this list is the complete dominance of European firms, with only two US-based firms (GE and Texas Utilities) accounting for US$ 35 billion-worth (9.6 per cent) of transaction value of this group. The dominance of European firms on the cross-border transaction league reflects the fact that global competition is requiring significant increases in size for European firms to compete with their larger US rivals.

M&A activities in the United States

At the same time, large American firms were also undertaking M&A activities, mostly with other American firms in the same industry (see Table 2.3). Among the 50 largest transactions involving US firms between 1980 and 2004, there were only six transactions involving European firms buying US assets in the same industry, accounting for 11 per cent of the total value of these transactions. Among the top 50 transactions with US firms as acquirers, the targets were all US firms. These are also industries that are active in cross-border transactions undertaken by large European firms.

Dominance of horizontal M&As

Horizontal M&As (between competing firms in the same industry) dominated the value of transactions, reflecting a strong trend among large firms to expand market share in their own industries. Among all cross-border transactions in 1999, the split among horizontal, vertical (between firms in client–supplier or buyer–seller relationships), and conglomerate M&As (between companies in unrelated activities) was 71 per cent, 2 per cent and 27 per cent respectively.[5] Among the 50 largest US transactions, 77 per cent by value were horizontal M&As, 11 per cent were spin-offs of non-core

Table 2.2   The 20 largest firms with cross-border M&A activity, 1987–99

Rank	Name	Country	Industry	Transaction Value (US$ billion)	No. of Deals
1	BP Amoco	UK	Petroleum	65.0	76
2	Vodafone	UK	Telecom	60.3	9
3	Mannesmann	Germany	Metal	44.7	44
4	DaimlerChrysler	Germany	Auto	42.9	67
5	Zeneca	UK	Chemicals	35.8	12
6	Aventis	France	Chemicals	26.8	13
7	Roche	Switzerland	Chemicals	24.7	20
8	Zürich Versicherungs	Switzerland	Insurance	21.9	36
9	GE	USA	Conglomerate	21.6	183
10	Seagram	Canada	Food and beverages	20.2	23
11	AXA	France	Insurance	19.1	44
12	Suez Lyonnaise	France	Electricity, gas and water distribution.	17.8	77
13	News Corp.	Australia	Media	17.4	64
14	Koninklijke	Netherlands	Conglomerate	17.5	301
15	AEGON	Netherlands	Insurance	17.1	22
16	Allianz	Germany	Insurance	16.9	72
17	Repsol	Spain	Oil and gas	16.4	24
18	Deutsche Bank	Germany	Banking	16.3	57
19	Hoechst	Germany	Chemicals	15.9	117
20	Texas Utilities	USA	Electricity, gas and water distribution.	15.7	18
Top ten				363.9	483
Top 20				533.8	1,279
Total				2,821.5	44,583

Source: UNCTAD, 2000: 127.

businesses to shareholders, 8 per cent were vertical M&As,[6] 2 per cent were financial buyouts, and 2 per cent were conglomerate M&As.

The dominance of horizontal M&As reflected the trend of large multinational firms to increasingly focus on their core businesses. The global business revolution witnessed a widespread narrowing of the range of business activity undertaken by the individual large firm. There took place massive asset restructuring, with firms extensively selling off 'non-core businesses' in order to develop their 'core businesses' and upgrade their asset portfolio. The goal for most large capitalist firms became the maintenance or

Table 2.3 Top 50 restructurings undertaken by US firms, 1980–2004

Date	Transaction value (US$ million)	Target name	Target nation	Acquirer name	Acquirer nation
1998	72,558	Citicorp	USA	Travelers Group	USA
1998	61,633	BankAmerica	USA	NationsBank	USA
2004	58,761	Bank One	USA	JP Morgan	USA
2003	49,261	FleetBoston	USA	Bank of America	USA
1998	34,353	Wells Fargo	USA	Norwest Corp	USA
1998	29,616	First Chicago	USA	BANC ONE	USA
2000	21,085	US Bancorp	USA	Firstar Corp	USA
1997	17,122	CoreStates Financial	USA	First Union Corp	USA
2001	23,398	American General	USA	AIG	USA
1998	22,300	General Re	USA	Berkshire Hathaway	USA
1998	18,117	SunAmerica Inc	USA	AIG	USA
2000	33,555	JP Morgan & Co Inc	USA	Chase Manhattan	USA
2000	30,958	Associates First Capital	USA	Citigroup Inc	USA
1997	26,625	Associates First Capital	USA	Shareholders	USA
Total financial services	499,341		25%		
2000	164,747	Time Warner	USA	America Online	USA
1998	53,593	Tele-Communications Inc	USA	AT&T Corp	USA
2001	47,041	AT&T Broadband & Internet	USA	Comcast Corp	USA
1999	44,779	MediaOne Group	USA	AT&T Corp	USA
2000	41,865	Liberty Media	USA	Shareholders	USA
1999	39,434	CBS Corp	USA	Viacom Inc	USA
1997	21,816	US WEST Media	USA	Shareholders	USA

Table 2.3 (Continued)

Date	Transaction value (US$ million.)	Target name	Target nation	Acquirer name	Acquirer nation
1995	18,837	Capital Cities/ABC	USA	Walt Disney	USA
Total media	432,111		22%		
1998	62,593	Ameritech Corp	USA	SBC Comm.	USA
1999	60,287	AirTouch	USA	Vodafone	UK
1998	53,415	GTE Corp	USA	Bell Atlantic	USA
1999	46,307	US WEST Inc	USA	Qwest Comm.	USA
2004	41,005	AT&T Wireless	USA	Cingular	USA
1997	37,407	MCI Communications	USA	WorldCom	USA
2000	24,404	VoiceStream Wireless	USA	Deutsche Telekom	Germany
1995	24,067	Lucent Technologies	USA	Shareholders	USA
1996	21,346	NYNEX Corp	USA	Bell Atlantic	USA
2000	21,101	Network Solutions	USA	VeriSign Inc	USA
2000	18,816	AT&T Wireless	USA	Shareholders	USA
Total telecom	410,748		21%		
1998	78,946	Mobil Corp	USA	Exxon Corp	USA
1998	48,174	Amoco Corp	USA	BP	UK
2000	35,872	Texaco Inc	USA	Chevron Corp	USA
1999	27,224	ARCO	USA	BP Amoco	UK
Total energy	190,216		10%		
2000	41,144	SDL Inc	USA	JDS Uniphase	USA
1999	31,180	Agilent Technologies	USA	Shareholders	USA
1995	27,974	Electronic Data System	USA	Shareholders	USA

2001	25,263	Compaq Computer	USA	Hewlett-Packard	USA
1999	21,423	Ascend Comm.	USA	Lucent Tech.	USA
2000	18,515	Seagate Technology	USA	Veritas Software	USA
1999	17,901	Palm Inc	USA	Shareholders	USA
Total technology	189,399		9%		
1999	89,168	Warner-Lambert Co	USA	Pfizer Inc	USA
2002	59,515	Pharmacia Corp	USA	Pfizer Inc	USA
1999	26,486	Pharmacia & Upjohn	USA	Monsanto Co	USA
Total pharmaceutical	175,169		9%		
1988	25,099	RJR Nabisco	USA	KKR	USA
2000	21,065	Bestfoods	USA	Unilever plc	UK
Total consumer	46,164		2%		
1998	40,467	Chrysler	USA	Daimler-Benz	Germany
Total auto	40,467		2%		
Total top 50	1,977,614		100%		

Source: SDC – M & A Data; Morgan Stanley.

establishment of their position as one of the handful of top companies in the global marketplace. The mantra for globally successful business became: 'If you're not number one, two or three in the world, you shouldn't stay in the business'. The 1990s saw an unprecedented period of merger and acquisition as leading firms divested themselves of non-core businesses, and acquired business units from other firms or merged with other firms in their sector to construct global businesses focused on a limited range of 'core businesses'. Although the intensity abated in the wake of the collapse of the late-1990s stock market bubble, the merger and acquisition process has continued at a high level in recent years.

Rise of global giants

The global business revolution at the end of the twentieth century has redefined the notions of *bigness* among capitalist firms. In 1959, the largest firm in the world was General Motors – it had US$ 11 billion in sales, US$ 7.9 billion in assets and employed over half a million workers. In 2003, the largest firm in the world was Wal-Mart; it had US$ 263 billion in sales, US$ 104 billion in assets and employed 1.5 million workers. At the end of the twentieth century, the 1,000 largest global firms accounted for 80 per cent of the world's industrial output, while the 300 largest firms controlled about 25 per cent of the world's productive assets (*Economist*, 29 January 2000). This dominance seems to have been increasing: in 1983, the revenues of the 200 largest firms were equivalent to 25 per cent of the world's GDP; by 1990, this percentage had increased to 27.5 per cent (Roach, 2005: 25).

The locations of these large capitalist firms are heavily concentrated in developed countries. In 2003, North America, Europe and Japan hosted 455, or over 90 per cent of the world's 500 largest corporations. Of the 100 largest corporations in the world, all but three are based in the United States, Japan and Europe (*Fortune*, 24 July 2004).

Industry concentration

It has now become clear that an unprecedented degree of industrial concentration at a global level has been established among leading firms in sector after sector. By the 1980s, there was already a high degree of industrial concentration within many sectors of the individual high-income countries (Pratten, 1971; Prais, 1981). However, the global business revolution saw for the first time the emergence of widespread industrial concentration across all high-income countries, as well as extending deeply into large parts of the developing world.

By the early 2000s, within the high value-added, high-technology, and/or strongly branded segments of global markets, which serve mainly the middle and upper income earners who control the bulk of the world's purchasing power, a veritable 'law' had come into play: a handful of giant firms occupied upwards of 50 per cent of the market share in the world's high value-added, high-technology, and/or strongly branded segments of global markets (see Table 2.4).

Table 2.4   Firm-level concentration in select global industries[a]

Industry	Number of top players	Combined global share (%)	Source
Aerospace			
Commercial aircraft over 100 seats	Top 2 firms	100	Morgan Stanley, 1998
20–90 seat aircraft	Top 2 firms	74	*FT*, Aerospace, 2000
Aero-engine orders	Top 3 firms	100	*FT*, 6 March 1998
Autos			
Automobiles	Top 6 firms	68	Morgan Stanley, 1999
Diesel fuel-injection pumps	Top 2 firms	73	*Ward's Auto World*, January 2000
ABS brake systems	Top 3 firms	72	*Ward's Auto World*, December 1997/*FT*, 8 May 1996
Tyres	Top 3 firms	51	*FT*, 19 January 1996
Complex equipment			
Gas turbines	Top 3 firms	87	*FT*, 24 March 1999
High-speed beverage bottling lines	Top 3 firms	85	Estimates by Krones and KHS websites
High-volume PET injection	Top firm	76	Husky, *Annual Report 2002*
PET blowing equipment	Top firm	55	Sidel, *Annual Report 1998*
Machine tool controls	Top firm	45	*FT*, 11 September 1996
Printing press	Top 4 firms	49	*FT*, 18 April 2000
Construction equipment	Top 4 firms	41	*FT*, 30 April 2004
Farm equipment	Top 3 firms	69	*FT*, 5 July 2000
Elevators	Top 4 firms	65	*FT*, 30 March 1999
Consumer electronics			
Digital cameras	Top 6 firms	80	*FT*, 15 December 2004
Electronic games	Top 2 firms	96	*FT*, 29 March 2000
LCD television sets	Top 3 firms	64	*FT*, 16 July 2004, 10 December 2004

Table 2.4   (Continued)

Industry	Number of top players	Combined global share (%)	Source
Flat screen television sets	Top 4 firms	55	*FT*, 12 June 2003
High purity glass for LCD screens	Top 2 firms	70	*FT*, 16 June 2004
Liquid crystals for LCD displays	Top 3 firms	95	*FT*, 29 May 2003
Large area TFT-LCDs	Top 5 firms	85	*FT*, 6 September 2004
Fast moving consumer goods			
Chewing gum	Top 2 firms	57	*FT*, 18 December 2002
Carbonated soft drinks	Top 2 firms	75	HBS case study 2002
Beer	Top 10 firms	>50%	www.oligopolywatch.com
Razors	Top firm	70	Morgan Stanley, 1998
Camera film	Top 3 firms	78	*Business China*, 30 July 2001
Tampons	Top firm	48	Morgan Stanley, 1998
Financial services			
Asset custodian	Top 4 firms	60	*FT*, 30 June 2003
Insurance brokerage	Top 3 firms	64	*FT*.com, 11 June 2001
Foreign exchange trading	Top 10 firms	64	*FT*, 17 May 2004
Accounting services	Top 4 firms	53	Gabel and Bruner (2003)
Equity underwriting	Top 10 firms	70	Morgan Stanley, *Annual Report 2004*
Debt underwriting	Top 10 firms	62	Morgan Stanley, *Annual Report 2004*
IT Hardware/Software			
ATM carriers for ISPs	Top 4 firms	84	*FT*, 6 June 2000
DSL	Top 2 firms	57	*FT*, 19 May 2001
Microprocessors	Top firm	80	*FT*, 3 December 2004
Semiconductors	Top 10 firms	50	Gabel and Bruner (2003)
Semiconductors for wireless communication	Top 10 firms	65	*IC Insights* www.icinsight.com
PC Operating systems	Top firm	85	*FT*, 29 April 2000
Word-processing applications	Top firm	90	*FT*, 24 June 1998
Business desktop computer applications	Top firm	90	*FT*, 29 April 2000

Database software	Top 3 firms	87	*FT*, 13 June 2003
Computerized reservations systems	Top 2 firms	68	*FT*, 23 June 1998
Computer routers	Top firm	66	Morgan Stanley, 1998
High-end routers	Top firm	80	Morgan Stanley, 1998
Optical fibres	Top firm	50	*FT*, 15 November 1999
Wireless network equipment	Top 3 firms	65	*FT*, 20 June 2006
DRAMs	Top 4 firms	76	*FT*, 2 September 2004
Hand-held computers	Top 2 firms	48	*FT*, 7 August 2001
Mobile phones	Top 4 firms	67	*FT*, 10 March 2003
Servers	Top 5 firms	85	*FT*, 23 December 2004
Smart cards	Top 3 firms	63	*FT*, 1 September 1999
Media			
Advertising	Top 4 firms	55	Merrill Lynch (2002)
Recorded music	Top 5 firms	80	www.oligopolywatch.com
Legal publishing	Top 3 firms	71	Merrill Lynch (2002)
Financial information	Top 2 firms	86	Merrill Lynch (2002)
Metals and mining			
Copper mining	Top 5 firms	53	Brook Hunt, Mining & Metal Industry Consultant, 2000
Steel (by value)	Top 7 firms	47	IISI
Stainless steel (by weight)	Top 2 firms	52	ThyssenKrupp, *Annual Report 2001–2002*
'Free market' aluminium supplies	Top firm	50	*FT*, 31 October 2001
Packaging			
Polyester film	Top firm	60	*FT*, 15 May 1998
Beverage cans (North America and EU)	Top 3 firms	85	CSFB, March 2004
Pharmaceutical			
Pharmaceutical sales	Top 10 firms	50	*FT*, 27 January 2004
Interventional therapy technologies	Top firm	45	Morgan Stanley, 1998
Artificial joints	Top 6 firms	90	*FT*, 21 May 2003
Other services			
Water management	Top 8 firms	68	Lehman Brothers (2002)
Cruise line berths	Top 2 firms	48	*FT*, 20 January 2002

Note: [a] These market shares are rough estimates only.

For example, estimates indicated that in most industrial sectors, by the early 2000s the global market share of the top three firms stood at 82 per cent in gas turbines (*FT*, 24 March 1999), 69 per cent in farm equipment (*FT*, 5 July 2000), 61 per cent in mobile phones (*FT*, 10 March 2003), and 51 per cent in LCD television sets (*FT*, 16 July 2004); the share of the top four firms stood at 63 per cent in the elevator industry (*FT*, 30 March 1999); the share of the top five firms stood at 82 per cent in digital cameras; the share of the top six firms stood at 70 per cent in the auto industry (Nolan, 2001a); and the share of the top ten firms stood at 50 per cent in the pharmaceutical industry (*FT*, 27 January 2004).[7]

Even in less well-known sectors, the share of system integrators has typically become very high. For example, the global market share of the top two firms in the financial information sector stood at 86 per cent (*FT*, 29 March 2000) and at 77 per cent in electronic games (Merrill Lynch, 2002); the share of the top three firms stood at 71 per cent in legal publishing (Merrill Lynch, 2002) and at 62 per cent in artificial joints (*FT*, 21 May 2003); the share of the top five firms stood at 77 per cent in recorded music; and the share of the top six firms stood at 60 per cent in water management (Lehman Brothers, 2002).

2.2   Systems integration and the emergence of the external firm

Penrose (1995) argued that management innovations, by effecting a progressive subdivision of function and decentralization of operations, have allowed large firms to continue to increase in size and influence without sacrificing efficiency. Over the course of the twentieth century, one may observe two major structural changes in business organization effected by large capitalist firms, facilitating optimal resource allocation decisions. The first is the adoption of the *multi-divisional* structure by large American firms in the first half of the century. The structure was created to answer new functions undertaken by integrated companies that not only manufactured goods, but also sold them, and purchased or even produced their own essential materials and other supplies (Chandler, 1990: 24–5). The global business revolution at the end of the twentieth century saw the rise of new management problems faced by the large capitalist firm and, as a result, witnessed the emergence of another management innovation by large capitalist firms: the practice of *systems integration* and creation of the 'external firm'.

New management problems

At the end of the twentieth century, increasing overseas operations have rapidly expanded the geographic scope of the large modern capitalist firm, which does business with foreign companies and/or operates subsidiaries in many countries. The global value chains of many industries are becoming increasingly complex. This is due to two reasons. First, the internationalization of capitalist firms has also coincided with an increasing technical complexity of products. Advances in engineering and innovations in production technology greatly increased the variety of products as well as the level of complexity in products. For example, the number of components has increased from 1,500 in 1920 to 30,000 in 2000 for automobiles, from 20,000 in 1945 to 3,500,000 in 2000 for aircraft, from 1,000 in 1970 to 100 million in 2000 for chip transistors. As a result, the amount of knowledge and resources required to design complete product systems has increased exponentially, and so has the number and range of technical specialties. An increasing amount of relevant technical knowledge starts to accumulate outside the core firm, requiring the firm to collaborate with a multitude of partners to research, design and manufacture its products.

The second factor has to do with the complexity of the global business environment itself. Kaplinsky and Morris underlined the complexity of the global business environment by pointing to 'the intricacy and complexity of trade in the globalization era', which

> 'requires sophisticated forms of coordination, not merely with respect to positioning (who is allocated what role in the value chain) and logistics (where and when intermediate inputs, including services, are shipped along the chain), but also in relation to the integration of components into the design of the final products, and the quality standards with which this integration is achieved'. (Kaplinsky and Morris, 2000: 29)

The value chains of seemingly simple products, such as a can of carbonated soft drink, have become incredibly complex. The Coca-Cola value chain spans a multitude of industries including steel, aluminium, glass, artificial sweeteners, farming, packing lines, bottle blowing equipment, injection moulding equipment, transportation logistics, retail, finance, etc. Coca-Cola must be able to facilitate cost reduction and technological progress of many of these industries in its value chain in order to increase the overall competitiveness of its global product. These improvements include lighter cans, cheaper, lighter and more durable glass bottles and improvements in transportation equipment. The skills involved in managing the Coca-Cola value chain are perhaps no less demanding than those involved in the manufacturing of complex product systems such as aircraft engines.

The increasing complexity of products, the rapid pace of technological change, and the increasing breadth of knowledge required to manufacture and deliver both consumer and capital goods globally have necessitated a new practice of organized economic production that transcends the boundary of firms. This management innovation is the practice of systems integration.

Systems integration

The concept of systems integration has its origins in military planning, production and procurement of the United States during the cold war, when the US military learned and helped its contractors to learn systems integration skills – the art of conceiving, designing and managing the development and deployment of large complex systems involving multiple disciplines and many participating organizations (Sapolsky, 2003; Gholz, 2003). The skills became central to the work of several aerospace firms, some government agencies and a few specially created non-profit organizations. Today, the task of systems integration is undertaken by large leading multinational firms in complex value chains. By the end of the twentieth century, in a wide range of business activities, the organization of the value chain has developed into a comprehensively planned and coordinated activity. At its centre is the 'systems integrator', or the core firm, which plays a critical function in planning, coordinating and regulating the activities within the value chain as a whole. This firm typically possesses some combination of a number of key attributes. These include the capability to raise finance for large new projects, and the resources necessary to fund a high level of R&D spending to sustain technological leadership, to develop a global brand, to invest in state-of-the-art IT and to attract the best human resources. This core firm functions as 'a spider in the industrial web that weaves, spins and manages the complex dependencies among the participants in the industrial complex' (Ruigrok and van Tulder, 1995: 65). The core firm has an explicit vision regarding both the internal structure of the value chain as well as the role that external actors should play to facilitate value creation (ibid.: 66).

As competition intensifies in global industries, systems integration has become one of the core capabilities that constitute the competitive advantage of many multinational firms. How well the core firm does against other global giants depends critically on its ability to coordinate and optimize the resources of other firms within its own value chain.

Dosi *et al.* (2003) underline the importance of knowledge in systems integration. They argue that the increasing modularity across components and the resulting specialization among firms in complex value chains have led to a need for additional integrative knowledge on the part of the systems integrator. As a result, the knowledge and production boundaries of the firm are likely to differ. In an analysis of the aircraft engines value chain, Prencipe (2003) observes that systems integration is primarily the ability to understand and integrate the different scientific and technological disciplines underlying the aircraft engine. Therefore, the integration of the aircraft engine is 'primarily seen as the integration of technological knowledge rather than the mere assembly of components' (ibid.: 121). Systems integration is, therefore, above all the integration of knowledge. Moreover, it involves the dynamic control of technological trajectories of the critical components and subsystems (Paoli, 2003). Such systems knowledge allows the systems integrator to set technical standards that play critical functions in coordination, negotiation and knowledge preservation in the value chain (Steinmueller, 2003).

In complex value chains, leading global firms with powerful technologies and marketing capabilities actively select the most capable among their numerous suppliers, in a form of industrial planning, as 'aligned suppliers' who could work with them across the world (Nolan, 2001a).

The relationship of the core systems integrator with the upstream first-tier suppliers extends far beyond the price relationship. Increasingly, leading first-tier suppliers across a wide range of industries have established long-term 'partner' or 'aligned supplier' relationships with the core systems integrators. There are some key aspects of the intimate relationship between systems integrators and upstream firms. First, leading first-tier suppliers plan the location of their plants in relation to the location of the core systems integrator. Second, it is increasingly the case that the aligned supplier produces goods within the systems integrator itself. It is common for leading suppliers of specialist services, such as data systems, to physically work within the premises of the systems integrator. Third, leading first-tier suppliers plan their R&D in close consultation with the projected needs of the core systems integrator. An increasing part of R&D is contracted out to small and medium-sized firms, typically under the close control of the systems integrator. Fourth, product development is intimately coordinated with the systems integrator. Finally, precise product specifications are instantaneously communicated to the leading suppliers through newly developed information technology. The production and supply schedules of leading first-tier suppliers are comprehensively coordinated with the systems integrator to ensure that the required inputs arrive exactly when they are needed and the inventory of the systems integrator is kept to a minimum.

Planning by systems integrators extends downstream also. Manufacturers of complex capital goods increasingly are interested in the revenue stream to be derived from maintaining their products over the course of their lifetime. New information technology is increasingly being used to monitor the performance of complex products in use, with continuous feedback to the systems integrator in order to construct optimum servicing schedules. Through this pervasive process, systems integrators deeply penetrate a wide range of firms that use their products. However, penetration of the downstream network of firms is not confined to complex capital goods. Systems integrators in the fast-moving consumer goods (FMCG) sector increasingly coordinate the distribution process with specialist logistics firms in order to minimize distribution costs. They work closely with grocery chains and other selling outlets, such as theme parks, movie theatres, oil companies (petrol stations have become major locations for retailing non-petrol products), and quick-service restaurants, to raise the technical efficiency in the organization of the selling process. The FMCG systems integrators often have their own experts working within the retail chain.

Emergence of the 'external firm'

Through systems integration, the core firms coordinate, appraise and plan activities of their value chain participants in a similar fashion to that in which the general office coordinates, appraises and plans activities at the division, departmental and field unit levels of Chandler's multi-divisional firm. In this respect, the visible hand of management has extended beyond the boundaries of the core firm to reach far-flung corners of the value chain. Through the hugely increased planning function undertaken by systems integrators, facilitated by recent developments in information technology, the boundaries of the large corporation have not only 'shifted', so that a wider range of goods and services is procured from outside the firm by purchase, but the very boundaries of the firms have become blurred. The core systems integrators across a wide range of sectors have become the coordinators of a vast array of business activity outside the boundaries of the legal entity in terms of ownership. The relationship extends far beyond the purchase price. In order to develop and maintain their competitive advantage, across a wide range of business types, from fast-moving consumer goods to aircraft manufacture, the systems integrators deeply penetrate the value chain both upstream and downstream, becoming closely involved in business activities that range from long-term planning to meticulous control of day-by-day production and delivery schedules. Competitive advantage for the systems integrator requires that it must consider the interests of the whole value chain in order to minimize costs across the whole system.

If we define the firm not by the entity which is the legal owner, but, rather, by the sphere over which conscious coordination of resource allocation takes place, then, far from becoming 'hollowed out' and much smaller in scope, the large firm can be seen to have enormously increased in size during the global business revolution. As the large firm has 'disintegrated', so has the extent of conscious coordination over the surrounding value chain increased.

A large corporation may have a total procurement bill of several billions of dollars. The procurement could involve purchases from numerous firms that employ a much larger number of full-time equivalent employees 'working for' the systems integrator than are employed within the core firm itself. A leading systems integrator with 100–200,000 employees could easily have the full-time equivalent of a further 400–500,000 employees 'working for' the systems integrator, in the sense that their work is coordinated in important ways by the core firm. In this sense, we may speak of an 'external firm' of coordinated business activity that surrounds the modern global corporation and is coordinated by it.

2.3   The cascade effect

One unique aspect of the global business revolution is the scope and intensity with which consolidation pressures affect entire supply chains. The process of concentration through simultaneous demerger of non-core businesses and merger of core businesses is cascading across the value chain at high speed.

While the systems integrator takes on increasing functions of planning and coordination within the value chain, it simultaneously delegates an increasing number of important activities to its suppliers and partners. In very complex systems, these delegated activities often include critical functions, such as the design, manufacturing and assembly of critical parts and subsystems. The capabilities of suppliers have therefore become an integral part of the competitiveness of the value chain and that of the systems integrator. In sector after sector, systems integrators have engaged in a form of industrial planning to cultivate a supply chain with *fewer*, but more *capable*, suppliers. This has substantially increased the requirements on the capabilities of these aligned suppliers and subsystems integrators in a wide range of areas including planning, R&D, financing, and service. As a result, systems integration by the core firm has created intense pressures for consolidation among the first-tier suppliers to expand capabilities and achieve economies of scale and scope in core businesses.

Thus, across a wide range of activities a 'cascade effect' is at work in which intense pressures develop for first-tier suppliers of goods and services to the global giants to themselves merge and acquire, and develop leading global positions. These first-tier suppliers and subsystems integrators, in their turn, pass on intense pressure upon their own supplier networks through the same process of systems integration. The result is a fast-developing process of concentration at a global level in numerous industries supplying goods and services to the systems integrators.

For example, in the auto industry, in the *Fortune 500* there are 13 giant auto components firms, with revenues of US$ 13–41 billion (*Fortune*, 2 August 2004). Each segment of the automobile is dominated by two or three of these giant subsystems integrators, including complete systems for brakes, transmission, electrical circuits, temperature controls, audio, glass, seats, and exhausts. They dominate the technologies of their respective sector. The world's top 700 companies ranked by R&D expenditure include 31 auto components suppliers, all headquartered in the high-income countries, with R&D expenditure ranging from US$ 82 million to US$ 2.9 billion. The R&D expenditure of the top five auto components firms ranges from US$ 630 million (ZF) to US$ 2.9 billion (Robert Bosch) (DTI, 2003: 62–4). In the following chapters we examine more examples of the cascade effect.

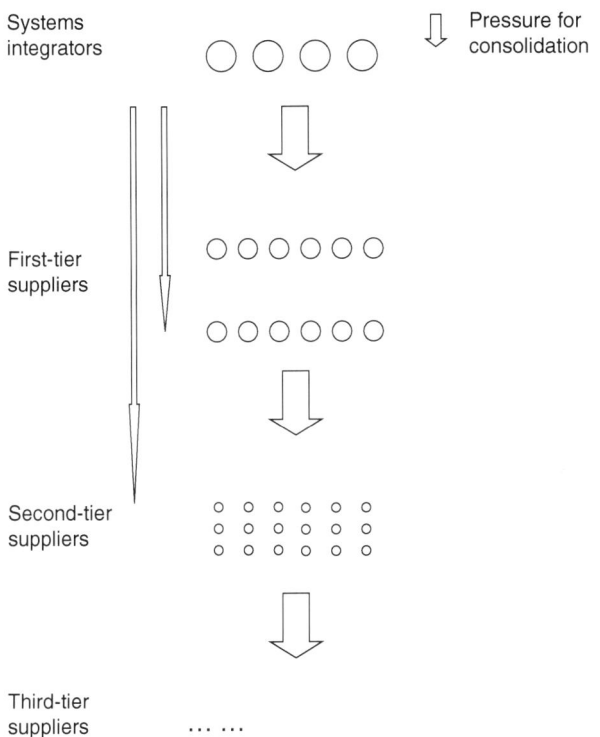

Figure 2.1 Cascade effect

Systems integrators sometimes establish direct relationships with second- or third-tier suppliers in a practice called 'upstreaming'. The systems integrator may purchase products or services directly from such lower-tier suppliers to establish control over the availability and/or quality of major system inputs and achieve transparency in the cost structure of intermediate products. For example, in many regions, Coca-Cola organizes procurement consortiums among its bottling partners in order to leverage enormous scale economies in procurement. The company is also directly involved in the purchase of plastic (PET) in order to control the price and quality of the raw materials for PET bottles, which are produced by second-tier suppliers in the system. The company has had a significant impact on the structure and growth pattern of the PET industry. For these lower-tier suppliers, therefore, the pressure for consolidation can often come directly from the systems integrator itself.

2.4   Summary

This chapter has briefly described the dramatic changes in the structure of global business at the end of the twentieth century. Large firms from high-income economies have grown even larger to dominate most of the high value-added industries in the global economy. The ever-increasing size of the capitalist firm did not bring about diseconomies of management. Continuous organizational innovations have allowed capitalist firms to continue to expand and dominate. The nature of capitalist competition has changed from domestic oligopolies to a handful of giant MNCs fighting over global market shares. Over 150 years ago, Karl Marx predicted this tendency towards industrial concentration and dominance of large capital, arguing for the 'laws of centralization of capitals' (Marx, 1867: 777). This process of concentration of capital first manifested itself in a fantastic fashion in the merger wave in the United States at the end of the nineteenth century. One may argue that this process was disrupted during the twentieth century by the two world wars and the cold war. As the disruptive forces faded away, the laws of centralization of capital have again manifested themselves in the global business revolution at the end of the twentieth century.

The global business revolution has also witnessed the emergence of systems integration by large core firms in managing complex global value chains. This management innovation, like the M-form structure before it, has helped large capitalist firms to continue to expand scale and influence without sacrificing efficiency. Under systems integration, the increased planning and coordination functions of the core firm with respect to its surrounding value chain have effectively blurred the boundary of the firm in a Coasian sense. As a result, business relationships in many of the world's high value-added industries can no longer be analysed as arms-length relationships. In these areas, the firm *versus* market dichotomy, so prominently featured in mainstream analysis, is quickly losing its validity.

Systems integration has not only profoundly changed the ways in which economic production is organized in the modern capitalist economy, but has also changed the structure of the productive mechanism, that is, the value chain itself. In sector after sector, the cascade effect has effectively increased the level of concentration at every important segment of the supply chain. The following three chapters examine the structural changes in the aerospace, beverage, and retail value chains during the global business revolution. They each seek to deepen understanding of the process of consolidation at the level of the systems integrator and in the surrounding supply chain.

3
The Aerospace Industry

Aerospace is considered by many countries as a strategic industry due to its critical importance in defence applications and the spill-over effect the industry creates for other high technology industries. During the past two decades, the global aerospace industry has undergone profound structural changes at every level of the aerospace value chain.

3.1 Consolidation of systems integrators

Large commercial aircraft and advanced military aerospace equipment contain bundles of the world's most advanced technologies. The design, assembly, marketing and upgrading of this equipment embodies powerful economies of scale and scope. The design of a new aircraft requires enormous investments with significant up-front costs during the launch stage. The development of the Boeing 787 is estimated to cost US$ 6–8 billion, while the development of the Airbus 380 is estimated to cost US$ 12–18 billion (*SCMP*, 29 March 2004). Meanwhile, these initial investments are highly risky, because the lead time to profit is very long. It typically takes four years from the decision to launch a new aeroplane to first delivery and another eight to ten years to recover launch cost. While the cost of failure is high, so is the reward for success. A successful new aeroplane could lock up its chosen market segment for as long as 20 years, producing sales of US$ 25–40 billion and huge profits. To this day, the Boeing 747, which almost bankrupted the company a few decades ago, has enjoyed a monopoly position in the >400 seat long-haul airliner market, bringing in US$ 45 million in gross profit on each aeroplane sold. In the history of the aircraft manufacturing industry, there had never been enough demand to ensure break-even profitability before the launch date. Due to the 'bet-the-firm' nature of new aircraft launches, every new aircraft design therefore requires extremely rigorous market analysis based upon the company's deep knowledge of its customers.

The industry has always benefited from economies of scale in assembly, which come from spreading planning efforts and high tooling costs over large outputs of one type of aircraft. In addition, there are economies achieved through learning effects, obtained in the course of producing more units of a given aircraft model. Boeing has developed 'learning curves' for machining, assembly and sheet metal fabrication, where each production run is scheduled for fewer labour hours to reflect the historical rate of learning on that operation (Simpson and Gavin, 1991).

In the aerospace industry, powerful economies of scale arise out of common platforms. Both Boeing and Airbus designed and manufactured aircraft in 'families'. The aircraft family strategy enables the manufacturer to spread given R&D outlays over a larger number of aircraft, and to obtain economies of scale in procurement of components, and to achieve large operating benefits. For both Airbus and Boeing, aircraft from the same family not only share a common fuselage and wing, they also have similar avionics systems, which help reduce training and operating costs (Nolan, 2001a). The aircraft family strategy also allows the learning effects to be applied to a larger number of aircraft.

Branding is also critical in the aerospace industry. For airline customers, the aircraft not only represents large capital outlays, but is also critical to safety, service quality and operating efficiency. A large installed base itself is in fact the best demonstration of product reliability, operating efficiency and technology leadership.

3.1.1 The global aerospace market

In both commercial and military aerospace businesses, which are closely related, the period since the 1980s has seen remarkable institutional change, leading to a high degree of industry concentration.

The market for the world's most expensive aircraft is enormous, offering the prospect of huge profits to the successful companies, whether in the commercial or military sector. Despite the downturn after 11 September 2001, there is still the prospect of a massive market for large commercial aeroplanes. The leading manufacturers estimate that between 2003 and 2020 there will be a market for around 24,000 commercial aeroplanes, with a total value of around US$ 2 trillion (at today's prices). Despite the restrictions on industrial consolidation in the sector,[8] airline privatization, the growth of large budget airlines, and the emergence of airline alliances, have placed intense pressure on commercial aircraft companies to cut prices while offering improved performance in terms of fuel efficiency, reliability and safety.

In the military aerospace sector, after the cold war, both the United States and Europe drastically reduced their defence spending (IISS, 1999: 37). Procurement techniques rapidly moved towards those of the civil aerospace world as governments pushed contractors to lower costs. Alongside the decline in defence procurement, European and US military aerospace manufacturers have been able to sell to markets that were inaccessible during the cold war (IISS, 1999: 283). September 11 had a huge impact on military spending in the world's largest market, the United States. In May 2003, the US Congress approved a US$ 400 billion defence budget for the year 2004. Moreover, the Pentagon's five-year defence plan forecasts increases of US$ 20 billion per year through to the end of the decade. The United States now spends more on its military than the next ten largest-spending nations combined (*FT*, 13 June 2003).

3.1.2   Consolidation in the United States

Commercial aircraft

Already, by the late 1960s, the US commercial aeroplane industry had reduced to just three main producers: Boeing, the world's leading manufacturer, producing a large 'family' of aeroplanes; McDonnell Douglas, the product of a merger in 1967, with a smaller 'family' of aeroplanes; and Lockheed, wholly reliant in the commercial arena on the L1011 Tristar. The competitive pressure from Boeing on its rivals was intense. By the mid-1990s, Lockheed had ceased production of the Tristar and McDonnell Douglas was in deep financial difficulties in its commercial aeroplane division. In 1997 came the path-breaking merger of Boeing and McDonnell Douglas. The resulting extraordinarily high level of industrial concentration received 'strong support from the US administration' (*FT*, 23 September 1997). This resulted in Boeing being the only producer of jet airliners in the United States. Following the merger, it accounted for 84 per cent of the world's total commercial aircraft in service (*FT*, 23 September 1997).

Military aerospace

Between 1994 and 1998 in the United States, there took place over US$ 62 billion-worth of mergers and acquisitions (*FT*, 3 September 1998). The Pentagon initiated the process over the famous 'Last Supper' in

1993. Between 1990 and 1998, the number of prime contractors for fixed-wing aircraft fell from eight to three; rotary wing aircraft four to three; tactical missiles 13 to four; expendable launch vehicles six to two; satellites eight to five; and, strategic missiles three to two (James, 1998). In this period, more than fifty companies were consolidated into today's 'Big five': Boeing, Lockheed Martin, Northrop Grumman, Raytheon and General Dynamics. The most significant event in this process was the merger between Boeing and McDonnell Douglas. After the merger, Boeing and Lockheed Martin completely dominated military aircraft sales to the US government. On 26 October 2001, the Pentagon awarded the US$ 200 billion Joint Strike Fighter (JSF) programme, the biggest-ever defence procurement, to Lockheed Martin. The procurement decision 'catapult[ed] Lockheed into an unassailable position as the world's top builder of fighter aircraft' (*FT*, 29 October 2001). Moreover, it is expected that over the lifetime of the JSF, the final cost will be several times that of the initial procurement, which could amount to up to US$ 1 trillion at today's prices. This was, arguably, the largest act of state industrial policy in history. The Big Five companies – Boeing, Lockheed Martin, Northrop Grumman, Raytheon and Honeywell – now account for 75 per cent of total sales in the sector, and each accounts for extremely high shares of individual segments of the market (Euromonitor, 2003a).

3.1.3   Consolidation in Europe

Commercial aircraft

In the 1950s and the 1960s, there were several European companies each manufacturing large (by the standards of the time) jet airliners. British firms manufactured the Comet (de Havilland), VC 10 (Vickers), Trident (Hawker Siddeley), and BAC 111 (BAC). West Germany manufactured the VFW 614, France produced the Caravelle, and the Netherlands made the Fokker. Although several of the aeroplanes were technically successful, by the late 1960s it was apparent that none of them was able to compete with the giants of the industry in the United States, especially Boeing. In 1970, in a critical and complex decision, France and Germany decided to join forces to build a family of large commercial aeroplanes that could challenge Boeing's dominance, and preserve a wide array of high-technology supplier industries within Europe. They were later joined by the United Kingdom and Spain. Although the precise amounts are disputed, there is no dispute that without massive support from the respective governments, Airbus could never have become established.

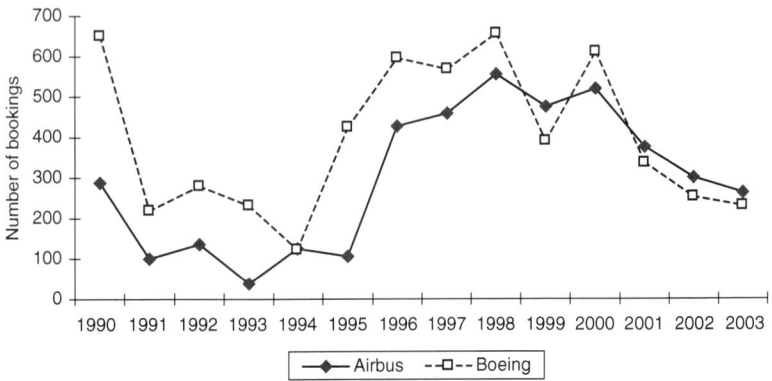

Figure 3.1   Commercial aircraft bookings by Boeing and Airbus since 1990
Source: Morgan Stanley Research, 10 December 2003.

Airbus has been an extraordinary long-term competitive success. It has created a complete 'family' of aeroplanes. By the early 2000s, it had firmly overtaken Boeing in the market for large commercial aircraft (see Figure 3.1). The two companies were now locked in head-to-head rivalry, each with their respective vision of the path of development of the commercial airliner industry in the decades ahead. Boeing has staked much of its future on the medium-sized 7E7, while Airbus has done the same with the super-large A380.

Alongside the dramatic rise of Airbus went the equally dramatic collapse of the once-powerful Soviet commercial aircraft industry. This highly sophisticated industry produced thousands of large jet passenger aeroplanes,[9] and with institutional change could have challenged the West's leading companies. Today, the industry is in ruins. The manufacture of large commercial aeroplanes is now truly a duopoly, but one with intense rivalry.

Military aerospace

Even before 11 September 2001, the total military budget in NATO Europe was less than one-half of that of the United States. The gap has become even wider since then. Moreover, most of the European military budget is spent by the individual national governments. The European military aerospace industry realized that it must unify or perish before the US challenge. Following a lengthy process of privatization, mergers and acquisitions within each of the larger European countries, the region finally took a dramatic step forward in October

1999, with the formation of the European Aeronautic Defence and Space Company (EADS). The constituent companies were Daimler Chrysler Aerospace (Germany), Aérospatiale Matra (France) and CASA (Spain). The new entity was a true giant to rival Boeing. Not only did it have an 80 per cent share of Airbus, providing over €19 billion euros in revenues, but also it had a powerful military division with revenues of over €5 billion in 2003 (EADS, *Annual Report 2004*). EADS has total revenues approaching US$ 40 billion, with expenditure of over US$ 5 billion on research and development.

3.1.4 Transatlantic mergers and acquisitions

The United States has the world's largest arms market by far. In an effort to prevent the emergence of a 'Fortress Europe' in the arms industry, the US government has been moving towards relaxing its controls on foreign investment in the industry and greater technology sharing with European-based defence firms. Jacques Gansler (the then Head of Procurement, Pentagon) announced that the Pentagon was willing to allow European or Asian companies to 'buy major US defence companies under certain conditions', one of which was that other countries must reciprocate, allowing similar access to their own markets (*IHT*, 8 July 1999). There have been increasing transatlantic acquisitions by both North American (United States and Canada) and European arms-producing firms. The number of major North American acquisitions of European arms-producing companies increased from five in 2001 to seven in 2002, while the number of European acquisitions of North American arms-producing companies increased from two in 2001 to seven in 2002 (see Table 3.1).

The 1990s also saw increases in programme-level collaborative arrangements between industrial firms. The JSF programme is by far the most significant. The United Kingdom is the sole Level 1 partner committing US$ 3.3 billion to the development costs and 'will be given a deeper insight into the workings of the F-35 [JSF] programme'. The Netherlands and Italy are the Level 2 partners, which will allow them to 'influence aspects of the F-35's design'. The Level 3 partners include Canada, Denmark, Norway, Australia, Singapore, Turkey and Israel. Level 3 partners will be given 'access to technical, cost and schedule data' so that 'they can shape their requirements around the aircraft' (*FT*, 22 July 2002). However, as a Level 1 partner, BAe Systems' demand for the source codes for the F-35 caused anger in the US administration. Without the source codes, the United Kingdom would have no autonomy to adapt the aircraft for operational requirements or perform

Table 3.1   Major transatlantic acquisitions of aerospace companies, 2001 and 2002

Buyer company (country)	Acquired company (country)	Seller company (country)	Price (US$ mil.)	Year
US/Canadian acquisitions of European companies				
Carlyle Group (USA)	BAe Systems unit (UK)	BAe Systems (UK)	200	2001
CAE (Canada)	BAe Systems unit (UK)	BAe Systems (UK)	80	2001
ONCAP (Canada)	BAe Systems Canada	BAe Systems (UK)	200	2001
FLIR Systems (USA)	Saab Tech Elecs unit (Sweden)	Saab (Sweden)	–	2001
General Dynamics (USA)	Santa Barbara (Spain)	(Spain)	5	2001
Carlyle Group (USA)	QinetiQ (UK)	UK government	220	2002
DRS Technologies (USA)	Meggitt subsidiary (USA)	Meggitt (UK)	–	2002
Esterline (USA)	BAe Systems unit (USA)	BAe Systems (UK)	68	2002
Herley Industries (USA)	EW Simulation (UK)	–	–	2002
Integrated Defense Technologies (USA)	BAe Systems unit (USA)	BAe Systems (UK)	146	2002
Kaman (USA)	RWG Frankenjura (Germany)	Privately owned	–	2002
One Equity Partners (USA)	HDW (Germany)	Babcock Borsig (Germany)	–	2002
European acquisition of US/Canadian companies				
Thales (France)	Magellan Corp (USA)	(USA)	70	2001
ASML (Netherlands)	Silicon Valley Group (USA)	(USA)	–	2001
GKN (UK)	Boeing unit (USA)	Boeing (USA)	5	2002
BAe Systems (UK)	Condor Pacific (USA)	–	59	2002

GKN (UK)	Astech (USA)	–	32	2002
Intra (Spain)	Intra EWS (Spain)	Raytheon (USA)	52	2002
Saab Barracuda (Sweden)	BAe Systems unit (USA)	BAe Systems (UK)	–	2002
Thales (France)	Sema (Germany)	SchlumbergerSema (USA)	–	2002
Ultra Electronics (UK)	CMC Electronics unit (Canada)	CMC Electronics (Canada)	34	2002

Source: SIPRI (2003).

important upgrades: 'Reprogramming the aircraft to face any future threats, ... could be done only once the US had given its permission' (*FT*, 14 July 2003).

3.2   Systems integration

Modern aircraft and engines have become so complex that a major aspect of competitive advantage has become the ability to integrate the whole system of supply to produce the final product. The systems integrators increasingly focus on the coordinating and planning function within the supply chain, rather than direct manufacture. As much as 60–80 per cent of the end-product value of aerospace products is now derived from the external supply network (Murman *et al*., 2002: 18). The system integrators have made large investments in IT systems, including mergers and acquisitions, in order to coordinate and control the supplier networks tightly with the core design and assembly location. This involves detailed, instantaneous exchange of information. For example, Airbus has more than 1,500 suppliers in 27 countries, including over 500 US companies. Boeing still has over 11,000 suppliers in 66 countries. The trend in both cases is to actively reorganize the supply chain in order to reduce the number of suppliers and nurture large-scale subsystems integrators. The way in which the industry leaders coordinate and reorganize the supply chain can be seen from the example of Boeing's lean manufacturing initiatives.

The demands from both airline customers and the US government have made cost control a critical component of Boeing's competitive strategy. In order to control costs, Boeing has implemented the principle of *lean manufacturing*, which includes the efficient use of assets, high inventory turns, short cycle times, high quality and low transaction costs.

This new philosophy has affected Boeing's design process, production operations and supplier management.

The design process

Eighty per cent of system cost in the aerospace industry is determined in the design phase. The number of parts, types of materials, processes, tooling approach, assembly techniques are the main drivers of cost and are established by engineers early in a system's life cycle. One of the key dimensions of lean manufacturing involved giving design teams the responsibility for cost. The design teams in turn aimed for simple designs with fewer and simpler parts that were easier to assemble and maintain. As a result, Boeing has been able to reduce cost substantially through fewer parts and lower tooling costs. As an example, the new design of the 767–400ER raked wing tip had 65 per cent fewer parts than the comparable 747–400 winglet. This resulted in 60 per cent fewer shims, 70 per cent less tooling cost, 44 per cent less fabrication time, and overall 30 per cent lower cost. On the military side, Boeing's design teams were able to reduce the number of parts on F/A-18E/F by 42 per cent compared to its predecessor F/A-18C/D, although the new aircraft was 25 per cent larger.[10]

As aircraft technology becomes more complex and the cost pressure increases, Boeing has been pushing more development and design activities down the supply chain to its subsystems integrators with each generation of new aircraft. In each aircraft programme, Boeing selects risk-sharing partners that develop and design important subsystems of the aircraft. Critical subsystems require massive R&D investments. For example, GE invested US$ 1.5 billion in the development of the GE90 for the B777, while the total R&D cost of the new B787 engine will reach US$ 1.2–1.5 billion. Boeing's top suppliers invest hundreds of millions of dollars in R&D every year (see Table 3.2). Most of the intellectual property in avionics is already developed and owned by a handful of top suppliers, as is most of the technology involved in aero engines. For suppliers, the growing R&D responsibility increases the expectation of their capabilities and sophistication. This requires not only greater investment and risk-taking but also closer collaboration with the systems integrator to maximize transfer of know-how and minimize technology risk.

Boeing's top suppliers are owning an increasing amount of intellectual property of the aircraft. The company believes that the increasing downward spread of R&D activities in the aerospace supply chain not only reduces technology risk for Boeing but also encourages innovation.

Table 3.2 R&D expenses by Boeing's main suppliers, 2003

Main suppliers	R&D expenses 2003 (US$ million)
Snecma	1,267
Honeywell	751
Rolls-Royce	500
GE	2,656*
United Technology	1,027*
Goodrich	312
Rockwell Collins	216
Alcoa	194
Parker Hannifin	122
Alcan	140

Source: DTI (2004).
Note: * R&D expenses of the whole company. R&D figures for the aerospace divisions are not available for GE and United Technology (Pratt & Whitney and Hamilton Sundstrand, respectively)

The manufacturing processes

In 2000, Boeing started to implement the Toyota Production System (TPS), converting its production system from batch processes to assembly line processes. Instead of going through the same production processes simultaneously on several planes, the new method called for a moving assembly line, which progressed forward at a speed of two inches per hour, putting physical pressure on factory workers to speed up work. The new manufacturing system identified production problems instantly and facilitated simplified flow of information within the plant. The TPS called for the collocation of engineers, support services and ordinary workers, which encouraged cross-fertilization of ideas to improve the system. The new system moved manufacturing R&D on-site to improve manufacturing technology. Unlike the batch method, TPS required just-in-time delivery of parts, which in turn called for changes in suppliers' operations.

Boeing also pushed more manufacturing and assembly activities down its supply chain. The manufacturing system at its Renton factory moved from an assembly of many discrete components to a final assembly of several pre-assembled subsystems. The change in manufacturing process allowed Boeing to decrease total labour needed in the whole supply chain while increasing efficiency. Boeing was able to adjust the production rate much more quickly, as tight collaboration with a handful of direct suppliers facilitated easier communication and coordination.

The new manufacturing system enabled Boeing to drastically reduce throughput time. After two years, Boeing reduced the throughput time for assembling a 737 from 13 days to seven days, and the throughput time for a 777 from 17 days to seven days. The reduction in throughput time reduced inventory and freed up a large amount of capital for Boeing and its supply chain partners.

Supplier management

Boeing's sharpened focus on cost reduction as well as the downward migration of development and manufacturing activities in the value chain required fundamental transformations in supplier management. As former Boeing CFO Mike Sears put it: 'If we are to succeed in the face of increasing global competition and greater demands for cost improvements from our customers, then *our entire extended enterprise* must operate under Lean principles and a Lean philosophy'.[11]

The first step in Boeing's new supplier management system was *supplier consolidation*. The Boeing Company spends more than US\$ 29 billion annually on procurement. In 1999, Boeing had as many as 30,000 suppliers, as each programme or manufacturing site did business with its local suppliers. In that year, Boeing's Supplier Management Process Council established 'strategic sourcing teams' (SSTs), which centralized the procurement function and reduced the number of suppliers. Strategic sourcing teams enable the Boeing business units to present a single company face to suppliers no matter what programme a supplier works with or where a supplier is located. There are nine SSTs categorized by nine commodity groups: avionics; electro/hydra/mechanical; major structures and platforms; purchased outside production/outside manufacturing; propulsion; aerospace commodities; interiors; aerospace support; and non-production commodities.

Five hundred experts work on these nine commodity-based SSTs. At the head of each SST is a team leader and an enterprise integrator, who work together to provide supply base data and analysis. Other members study their team's specific commodity needs or focus on the suppliers of that commodity. The SST leaders meet regularly to discuss supplier/commodity issues and share success stories. Each SST uses a detailed system of metrics to track supplier information, including costs, on-time delivery, quality acceptance.

The SMPC uses these supply base analyses to develop strategies to achieve cost reductions and enhance supplier performance. As a result, the total number of suppliers was reduced from nearly 30,000 in 1999 to 15,800 in 2002, 11,300 in 2003, and 10,800 in May 2004. In 2003, Boeing saved more than US$ 1 billion, 3.5 per cent of the total US$ 28.6 billion of the company's spending on procurement. In addition to cost reduction, the quality and performance of the Boeing supply base were improved. On-time delivery increased to 97 per cent from 88.7 per cent in 2001 and quality acceptance rose up to 99.9 per cent from 99.3 per cent in 2001 (Nolan and Zhang, 2004).

In order to better manage the performance of its suppliers, Boeing set out the Preferred Supplier Certification (PSC) programme, which evaluated suppliers through processes and performance in quality, technology improvements, delivery, costs and support. The SMPC set out the PSC process to evaluate a supplier's entire business operation. Boeing selects suppliers to participate in the PSC process through three types of evaluation:

- The 'Advanced Quality System' assessment evaluates suppliers' techniques in maintaining consistency and in improving quality and productivity of manufacturing and administrative processes.
- The 'Business Process' assessment evaluates suppliers in terms of product leadership, quality, delivery, costs, technology, and support. The assessment is conducted through on-site visits and interviews with supplier personnel. When the assessment is completed, the supplier submits to Boeing a continuous improvement plan 'to ensure its ongoing growth as a best-value supplier'.
- The 'Demonstrated Performance' assessment measures suppliers' performance in the areas of product delivery, quality, affordability, and customer satisfaction.[12] Suppliers who meet or exceed the standards in the above categories are identified and recognized as preferred suppliers.

Boeing has three levels of certification, 'bronze', 'silver', and 'gold'. Boeing's 'preferred suppliers' are entitled to additional benefits, including selection preference, reduced inspections, and additional business opportunities with other suppliers. By 2003, as much as 50 per cent of Boeing's annual procurement spending had been allocated to preferred suppliers, an increase from 41 per cent in 2002.

Boeing also pushed the procurement and supplier management function down the supply chain, reducing the number of direct suppliers with which it deals. During 2000–04, Boeing reduced its number of direct suppliers from 3,600 to 1,345. Its goal in 2005 was to reduce the number of direct suppliers to 1,200. In the supplier structure for the new 787, Boeing was to deal directly with only seven or eight first-tier suppliers. The reduction in the number of direct suppliers allowed Boeing to form closer collaboration with its direct suppliers and maintain tight control over the aircraft as technology and cost requirements continued to increase.

In order to induce its top suppliers to undertake more risk-sharing R&D activities, Boeing started increasingly to single-source its most valuable subsystems, where the small size of the market sometimes allowed survival of only one supplier. The trend towards single sourcing is most apparent in the aero engines segment. In the 777–300ER and 777–200LR programmes, the aircraft needed more thrust than any existing engine could supply. There was not a big enough market to sustain all three engine manufacturers, and as a result Boeing picked GE as the sole supplier, which subsequently developed the GE90 engine exclusively for the new planes. Another example of single sourcing is advanced composites, where innovation requires enormous investments. Toray is the sole supplier for advanced composites to B777 as well as B787.

Another important component in Boeing's supplier management was education. The company spent the last five to seven years on educating its suppliers on the concept of lean manufacturing. Boeing frequently hosted executive training classes to let suppliers 'know how we work and what we value'. The company also had more than 500 employees embedded in supplier organizations, including 50 'six sigma' black belts and 300 green belts. One of the most important functions of these embedded employees was to help the suppliers learn the principles of lean manufacturing, as one Boeing executive commented: 'some suppliers keep investing in machines and have the appearance of high technology. But this is more about processes than hardware. It is a learning process, like nurturing a child.'

Boeing executives believed that the 'lean enterprise' concept fundamentally changed the company's supplier management philosophy:

> our philosophy yesterday was to manage suppliers ruthlessly to lower costs – meet this cost target or we will switch suppliers. Today, Boeing is moving suppliers to the partnership column. We want them to succeed with us.

Boeing's journey towards becoming a 'lean enterprise' is comprehensively transforming its supplier base.[13] Boeing is penetrating deeply into its suppliers and closely monitoring their performance. Surrounding Boeing is a truly 'external firm'.

3.3   The 'cascade' effect in the aerospace value chain

In order to meet the demands of the systems integrators, the major components suppliers themselves need to invest heavily in research and development, and to expand in order to benefit from cost reduction through economies of scale and scope. A powerful merger movement is taking place among first-tier suppliers to the systems integrators.

3.3.1   Leading subsystems integrators

The enormous pressure for cost reductions in the civil and defence aviation markets caused Boeing to reshape its supply chains through supply base rationalization. The systems integrator now expected much more from a fewer number of suppliers in terms of subsystems integration, product innovation, services and cost reduction. Pressure from the systems integrator has driven prime suppliers to expand their capabilities through mergers and acquisitions, rapidly increasing the level of concentration at the level of subsystems integrators and key component suppliers.

As a result, large suppliers with significant R&D, financial and systems integration capabilities dominate every major subsystem of the aircraft, including aero engines, aero-structures and avionics and control systems. This group of large subsystems integrators includes such giant firms as United Technologies (revenues of US$ 31 billion and profits of US$ 1.3 billion), Honeywell (US$ 23 billion revenues), Textron (US$ 10 billion), Snecma (US$ 7.3 billion), Parker Hannifin (US$ 6.4 billion), L-3 Communications (US$ 5 billion), Goodrich (US$ 4.4 billion), Rockwell Collins (US$ 2.5 billion), Alliant Techsystems (US$ 2.1 billion), Precision Castparts (US$ 2.2 billion) and Smiths Industries (US 4.9 billion) (see Table 4.6; and *Fortune*, 5 April 2004). All of these suppliers are headquartered in, and have their main production facilities in developed countries, especially the United States. All have collaborated with Boeing for decades, competing and collaborating with each other in every aircraft programme. Leaders in their respective industries, all are global giants themselves with billions of dollars in revenues.

Through continuous merging and acquiring 'core businesses' that meet their strategic goals, and through divesting 'non-core businesses' in order to 'upgrade' their asset portfolio, these giant subsystems integrators have established or strengthened their competitive position in businesses covering one or more aircraft subsystems.

- *Vought Aircraft.* Vought Aircraft (currently owned by the Carlyle Group) is a major supplier of integrated airframe structures. In 2003, the company had a turnover of US$ 1.2 billion and 6,000 employees. In July 2003, Vought Aircraft Industries purchased The Aerostructures Corporation. Vought has work shares on almost every Boeing jetliner in production, from the 737 to the 777. For example, since the beginning of the 747 in 1968, Vought has built the 747's major structures, including the main fuselage section, doors and the tail section. The fuselage is the largest single subcontract on the 747 aircraft. It consists of 28 major panels and includes 11 doors and 110 floor beams. The 747 tail section includes the aft body section, the vertical and horizontal stabilizers, rudders and elevators. By July 1993, Vought had delivered the 1,000th tail section for the Boeing 747. In July 2004, Vought delivered the last of the 1,050 ship sets to Boeing for the completion of the 757 programme. In November 2003, Vought was selected as a structural supplier on the Boeing 7E7 programme. Vought and Alenia Aeronautica of Italy are teaming up on work packages, which together account for approximately 26 per cent of the 7E7 structure. Vought also is one of the largest structures suppliers to Airbus. It provides various wing components, some measuring more than 100 feet long, for the A319/320 and A330/A340–300–500–600 families. In 2004, the company delivered the 500th A319/A320 wing component.
- *BAe Systems.* BAe Systems owns 20 per cent of Airbus (Airbus UK). Through its two sites, Broughton and Filton in the United Kingdom, Airbus UK designs and produces wings for all Airbus families. By July 2004, Airbus had delivered 3,617 jetliners, of which 2,241 are for the A320 family, 786 are for the A300/A310 family and 590 for the A330/A340 family: they all have wings supplied by BAe Systems.
- *GE/Rolls-Royce/Pratt & Whitney.* Engines are by far the most expensive aircraft subsystem. There are powerful economies of scope in engine development, because the giant producers each has a 'family' of similar engines. However, the investment required for an engine for a new model of aeroplane is enormous. For example, GE invested US$ 1.5 billion to develop the GE 90 for the Boeing 777 (Nolan, 2001a: 172). The leading engine manufacturers must invest large sums in R&D if they are to meet their customers' stringent requirements for fuel efficiency, safety, noise, and reliability. For example,

Rolls-Royce spends over US$ 500 million per year on R&D (DTI, 2003: 62). There are now only three engine makers left that have the capability to produce large modern jet aircraft engines, namely Rolls-Royce, Pratt & Whitney of United Technology and GE Engine of GE. By the late 1990s, the respective shares of aircraft engine orders for large passenger jets was 53 per cent for GE, 34 per cent for Rolls-Royce, and 13 per cent for Pratt & Whitney (Nolan, 2001a: 172).

- *Honeywell.* The Allied Signal/Honeywell merger in 1999 created Honeywell International (Honeywell), a company that has 'a strong position in everything from manufacturing cockpit controls to handling aircraft service and maintenance' (*FT*, 8 June 1999). In 2002, Honeywell acquired Invensys' sensor systems for US$ 416 million in cash, further strengthening its capabilities in electronic systems.

- *Smiths Industries Aerospace.* Smiths has built a leading position in the control and management of aircraft utilities, and in electrical, mechanical and hydraulic systems through a series of acquisitions during the 1990s. In 2000, Smiths made 11 acquisitions, including the aerospace division of Invensys, the actuation division of BAe Systems. Through the merger with the TI Group in the same year, Smiths strengthened its first-tier aerospace supplier status by integrating Dowty of the TI group.

- *Goodrich.* Between 1986 and 2002, Goodrich completed 56 mergers and acquisitions,[14] 41 of which were in the aerospace sector. In 2001, Goodrich acquired Heller Aerospace Lighting, manufacturer of aerospace lighting systems and related electronics, and Humphrey Inc., designer and manufacturer of inertial sensors used for guidance and control of unmanned vehicles and precision-guided systems. In 2002, Goodrich bought from Northrop Grumman the TRW Aeronautical Systems for US$ 1.4 billion. The whole company has been reorganized into three business segments, covering engine, electronic, landing, actuation, and flight control systems.

- *Rockwell Collins.* Following its spin-off from Rockwell International in 2001, Rockwell Collins completed three major acquisitions to strengthen its capabilities in avionics systems. In March 2002, it acquired Communication Solutions Inc., for signals intelligence and surveillance solutions, Airshow Inc., for cabin electronics systems in August 2002 and NLX-LLC, a leader in integrated training and simulation systems, in October 2003.

- *Parker Hannifin.* Between 1991 and June 2004, Parker Hannifin completed 55 mergers and acquisitions, averaging four acquisitions each year. In 2000, the company acquired Dana Corporation's hydraulic business and Commercial Intertech Corp.

- *Snecma.* Through a series of acquisitions, Snecma assembled a group of companies in engine, landing, and electrical/hydraulic systems. In 1998, Snecma acquired the landing gear company Messier-Dowty. Messier-Dowty is one of only two companies in the world capable of producing landing gear for large jets of over 100 seats capacity. According to Snecma, its Messier-Bugatti subsidiary accounts for 35 per cent of the market for carbon brakes on jetliners of over 100 seats, compared with 35 per cent market share for Goodrich. In the braking control systems market, Messier-Bugatti is the sole source supplier to Airbus, while Crane-Hydroaire of the United States is a sole supplier to Boeing. Snecma is the only manufacturer in the world to offer both wheels and brakes and braking control systems for mainline jets. In 2000, Snecma acquired Labinal, the world leading company in aircraft wiring.

3.3.2 Niche subsystems integrators

There is also a group of smaller subsystems integrators that have assembled capabilities in niche segments of the aeroplane, such as Zodiac Group electronic and electrical/hydraulic subsystems, Cobham and Meggitt in components for electronic, landing, and electrical/hydraulic systems, B/E Aerospace and JAMCO in inserts.

- *Zodiac Group.* Since the acquisition of Air Cruisers in 1987, the Zodiac Group has acquired numerous other European and international companies such as Pioneer (1988), Weber Aircraft (1992), MAG Aerospace (1998), Intertechnique (1999), Esco (2002), and Icore (2003). Today, the Zodiac Group has 60 subsidiary companies worldwide. The acquisition of Esco has enabled Zodiac to become the world leader in aircraft emergency arresting systems, while the purchase of Icore makes Zodiac one of the two world leaders specializing in airbags. Zodiac also provides system integration in cabin waste and water management and galley refrigeration.
- *Cobham.* Between 1995 and 2003, Cobham acquired 43 companies, compared with two divestitures. In 2003, Cobham made 13 acquisitions, nine of which are for the avionics sector and three for aerospace systems. Through continuous acquisitions, Cobham has assembled a complementary range of niche products and systems for the civil and defence aviation, marine, search and rescue, aerospace and communication markets.

- *Meggitt*. The trend towards concentration is also affecting smaller companies within the industry with very small niche positions, with specific technologies to enable them to have a high global market share in the niche. Through its acquisition of Whittaker Corporation, Meggitt was able to supply valves, ground fuelling products and fire and smoke detectors to 'virtually every aircraft maker in the West' (*FT*, 10 June 1999). The merger was explicitly driven by the assemblers' push to reduce the number of parts suppliers.

- *Interiors*. The aircraft interior equipment has increasingly become a focal point of airlines' marketing strategy. Moreover, a new international safety standard known as 16G has been introduced, which requires cabin-equipment materials to be able to withstand a crash impact 16 times the force of gravity. This requires that firms have the technical and financial capabilities to meet tougher constraints in design, manufacturing and maintenance. There has been a growing concentration among interior equipment suppliers, with B/E Aerospace, Zodiac, C&D Aerospace, JAMCO, and Recaro Aircraft Seating (Putsch Group) as the world's leading firms.

- *B/E Aerospace*. Seats account for approximately 50 percent of the cost for cabin interior. A first-class seat consists of around 3,000 components, ranging from textile and leather to fine metal sheet, plastics and electronics. Since 1989, B/E Aerospace has completed 24 acquisitions, amounting to approximately US$ 1 billion, around one half of which were for seating system and galley equipment. B/E has an installed base of more than one million seats in service. B/E is the world's largest and only fully integrated manufacturer of food and beverage preparation and storage equipment for commercial and business jet aircraft. In addition, B/E is the only manufacturer with the capacity to manufacture and fully integrate oxygen equipment with passenger service units.

- *Recaro Aircraft Seating*. Germany's Recaro Aircraft Seating is Boeing's preferred supplier in seating products and supplies economy and business class seats for many major airliners. In 1997, the company won a contract to supply 36,000 economy seats for American Airlines. It subsequently had major orders from Lufthansa, Swissair, Scandinavian Airlines and Alitalia. In 1999, Recaro developed the 'World Traveller Plus' for British Airways, a new class of seats between economy and business class.

- *JAMCO*. JAMCO supplies lavatories for all the Boeing 717, 747, 767, and 777 series, amounting to more than 3,400 aircraft. It also supplies over 200 airliners with galleys and inserts. The galley and inserts parts require high quality as well as weight reduction.

3.3.3 Materials and major components

The trend of consolidation does not stop at the level of subsystems integrators and major component suppliers, which pass along the same pressures in cost reduction, increased product development and service capabilities to their own respective supply chains. A senior executive of a tier-1 aerospace supplier commented, 'Our vision is to develop a low-maintenance supply chain made up of partnerships with large scale, innovative companies who have a strategy to develop and grow their business'.[15] Smaller and weaker suppliers are either acquired by larger and stronger ones or have to accept a lower position in the supply chain; sometimes they are eliminated from the global supply chain altogether. Such is the 'cascade effect' that is taking place in many of today's global value chains.

- *Alcoa/Alcan.* Until the most recent developments in composites, aluminium was the most important material used in the construction of aeroplanes. Even with the new generation of composites, such as on the 7E7, aluminium is still extremely important in aircraft construction. Alcoa and Pechiney have for decades been the industry leaders in the highly specialized field of supply of aluminium panels and aluminium components to the aerospace industry. Alcoa has consistently been in the number one position globally, with the leading position in the US market. Alcoa and Pechiney have closely collaborated with the world's leading aerospace manufacturers and engine makers, both commercial and military, to achieve technical progress in the supply of aluminium, as well as alloys and titanium products for aircraft. By 2003, Alcoa's revenues from aerospace alone totalled US$ 2 billion. Its aerospace division has 5,500 employees working in 26 plants worldwide. No other aluminium companies come close to the importance of Alcoa or Pechiney in supplying the aerospace industry, or in collaborating with the leading manufacturers in achieving technical progress. In 2003, Pechiney was taken over by Alcan (Canada), which formerly had no significant position in supplying the aerospace industry.
- *Michelin/Goodyear/Bridgestone.* Today, these three firms are giants of the automobile components industry. They have each grown through a long series of mergers and acquisitions since the 1980s, to become the world's leading tyre makers, with revenues of between US$ 15 billion and US$ 20 billion (*Fortune*, 26 July 2004). Between them, they produce around 60 per cent of the world's tyres.

However, there is a wide variety of tyres. These companies specialize in the production of high-technology, high value-added tyres. They spend between US$ 400 million (Goodyear) and US$ 830 million (Michelin) on research and development (DTI, 2003: 62). This enables their tyres to have superior, and continually advancing capabilities in terms of safety, contribution to fuel efficiency, durability, and ability to withstand violent impact. These attributes are even more important on aircraft tyres than in those for automobiles. These giant companies benefit from substantial economies of scope in research and development, which permits them to be the global leaders in tyres for large aircraft as well as automobiles. In the early days of the aircraft industry, there were innumerable suppliers of aircraft tyres. Today, there are no competitors other than the three tyre industry giants, for the supply of tyres to large commercial aircraft. Concentration in the systems integrators has been closely accompanied by concentration in one of the most important components.

• *Saint-Gobain*. Since the 1970s, Saint-Gobain has built itself into a global giant of the glass industry, mainly through a long stream of mergers and acquisitions. It has global leading positions in many different types of glass products. As a state-owned firm, it benefited from being the sole supplier to Caravelle, the aircraft maker, which was also a French 'national champion'. Following its privatization, it was able to build on its already strong position in the sector, to establish itself as the only firm in Europe with the technical capability to meet the fast-advancing needs of leading aircraft makers for glass for cockpits, cabins doors and passenger windows.

3.3.4 Maintenance, repair and overhaul

Due to the long life of an aircraft, maintenance, repair and overhaul (MRO) operations (i.e., after-sales service,) are a particularly lucrative part of the aerospace value chain. For example, analysts estimate that while the new Boeing 787 will bring in US$ 11–12 billion in revenues for suppliers, the after-market revenues could run to as much as US$ 70 billion (*FT*, April 11, 2004). In 2002, the worldwide commercial jet MRO market is estimated to be as large as US$ 37.8 billion (Find/SVP, 2002). In North America, about 75 per cent of MRO services are performed in-house by the major airline carriers. Smaller carriers do not have the scale to provide the same array of MRO services and have to rely on airline alliances or outsource MRO work to third-party providers. Independent maintenance companies hold 15 per cent of the market and original equipment manufacturers (OEMs) hold 10 per cent. Consolidation among airlines and competition from OEMs have created pressures for consolidation in the MRO sector. To compete effectively with the larger airlines and the OEMs, third-party MRO firms will have to offer a wide array of services with greater geographical coverage. It is expected that the number of providers will decrease over the next few years as smaller players leave the market or merge into larger entities (AT Kearney, 2003).

Table 3.3   M&A activities among major subsystems integrators in Boeing's supply chain

Subsystems integrator/sales (US$ billion)	Merger and acquisition activities
Aero-engines GE Aircraft Engines (USA)/11	• 1997: acquisition of Greenwich Air Services and Garrett Aviation services, a leading provider of engine overhaul services in the United States • 1999: acquisition of ElectroSonics, a provider of avionics services headquartered in Columbus, Ohio • 2002: acquisition of Unison Industries, a world leader in the design and manufacture of electrical and mechanical components, sensors, and systems for aircraft, industrial, marine, military, and space uses. In the 1990s, Unison designed and provided ignition and electrical power systems for over 90 per cent of all new aircraft produced. Prior to GE's acquisition, Unison had purchased AlliedSignal's Bendix Aircraft Ignition business (1989), BF Goodrich's Engine Electrical Systems Division (1997), and Westport International (2000) • 2005: acquisition of Agfa-Gevaert's non-destructive testing business unit to form the GE Inspection Technologies
Pratt & Whitney (USA)/7.5	• 2000: acquisition of Cade Industries, a global leader in the design, manufacture and service of jet engine test facilities and ground testing equipment • 2000: acquisition of the engine maintenance centre of Braathens ASA, strengthening P&W's engine overhaul capabilities • 2000: acquisition of Space Power Inc.
Rolls-Royce (UK)/ 10.4	• 1995: acquisition of Allison Engine, which helped R-R to establish a strong presence in regional aircraft engines

- 1999: acquisition of Vickers for £576 million, transforming R-R into a global leader in marine power systems
- 1999: acquisition of Cooper Energy; and acquisition of National Airmotive, a provider of engine repair and overhaul services
- 2003: acquisition of VT Controls, expanding R-R's presence in marine electrical systems

Snecma (France)/ 7.27

- 1998: acquisition of Messier-Dowty, one of the only two companies in the world capable of producing landing gear for large jets
- 2000: acquisition of Labinal, the world leading supplier in aircraft wiring

Aerostructures

Vought Aircraft (USA)/1.2

- July 2003: purchase of The Aerostructures Corporation

BAe Systems (UK)/16.1

- 1996: acquisition of AWA Defence Industries (AWADI), an Australian defence company for A$ 50million
- 1997: acquisition of Reflectone, manufacturer of flight simulators; £90 million acquisition of 49 per cent of STN Atlas Elecktronik, the German systems integration business, 30 per cent interest in German guided weapons business LFK, a subsidiary of Daimler-Benz Aerospace
- 1998: acquisition of Siemens Plessey Systems, and 35 per cent interest in Saab AB
- 1999: merger with GE's Marconi Electronic Systems
- 2000: acquisition of two divisions of Lockheed Martin for US$ 3 billion
- 2003: acquisition of Advanced Power Technologies, Alvis, APTI, and MEVATEC
- 2004: acquisition of Alphatech, which specializes in image and signal processing and intelligent systems for the DOD, for US$ 84 million; DigitalNet for US$ 600 million; Practical Imagineering, a provider of digital signal processing systems and software research and development, for US$ 8.3 million
- 2005: acquisition of United Defense (USA) for US$ 3 billion

Avionics and control systems

Honeywell (USA)/ 9.0

- 1997: acquisition of Grimes Aerospace, which established Honeywell's leadership position in aircraft lighting
- 1999: merger between AlliedSignal and Honeywell International to create the world's leading avionics company

Table 3.3   (Continued)

Subsystems integrator/sales (US$ billion)	Merger and acquisition activities
Rockwell Collins (USA)/2.5	• March 2002: acquisition of Communication Solutions, for signals intelligence and surveillance solutions • August 2002: acquisition of Airshow for cabin electronics systems • October 2003: acquisition of NLX-LLC, a leader in integrated training and simulation systems
Smiths Industries Aerospace (UK)/4.9	• 2000: 11 acquisitions, including Invensys, actuation division of BAe Systems • 2000: merger with the TI Group (integrating Dowty)
Goodrich (USA)/4.4	• 1986–2002: completed 56 mergers and acquisitions, 41 of which were in the aerospace sector • 2001: acquisition of Heller Aerospace Lighting, manufacturer of aerospace lighting systems and related electronics • 2001: acquisition of Humphrey, designer and manufacturer of inertial sensors used for guidance and control of unmanned vehicles and precision-guided systems • 2002: US$ 1.4 billion acquisition of TRW Aeronautical Systems from Northrop Grumman
Parker Hannifin (USA)/6.2	• 1991–2004: completed 55 mergers and acquisitions • 2000: acquisition of Dana Corporation's hydraulic business and Commercial Intertech
Hamilton Sundstrand (USA)/ 3.6	• 1996: acquisition of Dynamic Controls Corp., a leader in the design and development of electronic and electro-mechanical controls and systems; APIC, the auxiliary power unit joint venture, from Labinal • 1998: acquisition of Ratier-Figeac of France, a major manufacturer of aviation components; four other acquisitions include Williams Instrument, the gear products business of A. Goninan (Australia), and two pump manufacturers – ANSIMAG and MASO Process Pumpen (Germany) • 1999: acquisition of Sundstrand, and IMI Marston's Aerospace Heat Transfer and Fluids Management business • 2001: acquisition of Claverham Group, a UK-based supplier to the European defence industry, Sensor Systems Division of Orbital Sciences, and commercial aviation maintenance and repair organization Caribe

Table 3.4 Select suppliers of niche subsystems, major components and materials in Boeing's supply chain

Subsystems integrator	Country	Revenues (US$ billion)	Niche subsystems	Merger and acquisition activities
Zodiac Group	France	1.7	Aircraft emergency arresting systems; airbags; cabin waste and water management; galley refrigeration	• 1987–92: acquisitions of Air Cruisers, Pioneer, and Weber Aircraft • 1998: acquisition of MAG Aerospace • 1999: acquisition of Intertechnique • 2002: acquisition of Esco, a leading supplier of aircraft emergency arresting systems • 2003: acquisition of Icore, one of the two world leaders in airbags
Cobham	UK	1.6	Avionics subsystems; specialized aerospace components, including life support, refuelling, fluid and air countermeasures	• 1995–2003: acquired 43 companies • In 2003: made 13 acquisitions, nine of which are for the avionics sector and three for the aerospace systems • 1989–2004: made 24 acquisitions amounting to about US$ 1 billion, around half of which were for seating system and galley equipment
B/E Aerospace	USA	0.62	Seating system; galley equipment; food and beverage preparation and storage equipment; oxygen equipment and passenger service units	
JAMCO	Japan	0.29	Lavatories; galleys and inserts	• NA

Table 3.4 (Continued)

Subsystems integrator	Country	Revenues (US$ billion)	Niche subsystems	Merger and acquisition activities
Recaro	Germany	NA	Economy and business class seats	• NA
Meggitt	UK	NA	Valves; ground fuelling products; fire and smoke detectors	• 1999: acquisition of Whittaker Corporation, a leading supplier of valves, ground fuelling products and fire and smoke detectors
Michelin	France	18.1	Aircraft tyres	• 1996–2001: four acquisitions including Taurus (Hungary) in 1996, a majority stake in Kronpinz (Germany) in 1997, Icollantas (Colombia) in 1998, and two Tofan factories (Romania) in 2001
Goodyear	USA	15.1	Aircraft tyres	• 1995–2004: eight acquisitions including majority control of TC Debica (Poland) and Air Springs (Brazil) in 1995; 50 per cent stake in Dackia (Sweden), Sime Darby Pilipinas (Philippines), 60 per cent interest in Contred (South Africa) in 1996; Belt Concepts (USA) in 1996; Indomax (Venezuela) in 1997; South Asia Tyres (India) in 1998
Bridgestone	Japan	19.9	Aircraft tyres	• 1994–2004: three acquisitions, including 50 per cent stake in Hong Kong Aircraft Engineering Co. in 2000; Shenyang Santai Tire Co. Ltd. (China) in 2000; a 19 per cent stake in Nokian (Finland) in 2003
Alcoa	USA	21.7	Aluminium panels and components	• 1994–2002: 21 mergers and acquisitions, including Alumax, Inespal (Spain) in 1998; Reynolds' Extrusion Plant in Spain in 1999; Midwest Fastener Corporation (USA), Baco Consumer Products (UK), Southern

Company	Country		Products	Acquisitions
				Plastics (USA), Cordant Technologies (USA), Reynolds Metals (USA), MCG Closures Limited, Howmet International (USA), Noyes in 2000; LTDREDD Team, North American Metals (Canada), Laser Armor Tech Corporation, ISAC Corporation in 2001; Noranda Aluminum (USA), Fairchild Fasteners, Ivex Packaging Corporation (USA), Dooray Air Metal (Korea), Engineered Plastic Components, Elkem (Norway) in 2002
Alcan	Canada	13.6	Aluminium panels and components	• 1995–2003: four acquisitions, including Alsuisse Group (Switzerland) in 1999, Pechiney (Australia), VAW Flexible Packing (Germany), Baltec and Uniwood/Fome Corp. in 2003
Saint-Gobain	France	33.5	Glass for cockpits, cabin doors and windows	• 1995–2004: 13 acquisitions, including Ball Foster Glass (USA) in 1995, Polliet (France) in 1996, GS Roofing (USA) in 1999, Quartz International (USA) in 1999, Biwater Industries (UK) and Raab Karcher (Germany) in 2000, Baywa (Czech Republic) and Keramundo (Germany) in 2001, PUM Plastiques (France), Dubois Matériaux (France) in 2003, Sanitas Troesch (Switzerland), Plafométal (France), Dahl International (Scandinavia) in 2004

3.3.5   Major suppliers for the Airbus A380 and Boeing 7E7

In the commercial aircraft sector, the Airbus A380 and Boeing's 7E7 are the two most important programmes for at least the next two decades as are the A400M and the Joint Strike Fighter (JSF) in the military aircraft sector. All of the four programmes involve massive investment and represent highly sophisticated technology. Boeing reported its 7E7 partner team including 15 companies from at least ten US states and seven countries. About 70 per cent of the content by value, excluding the engines, will come from the United States (*FT*, 19 July 2004). For the A380, Airbus holds about 180 major contracts with more than 100 different suppliers and industrial partners, among which only one company is from a developing country.[16]

The Boeing 7E7 and the Airbus A380 each has a group of giant suppliers that are heavily involved with one programme but have a smaller role on the other:

- *Boeing 7E7*. Engine suppliers are Rolls-Royce, and General Electric. The work share on the main structural sections of the 7E7 has been divided mainly between the United States, Japan and Italy. Japan will produce 35 per cent of the airframe including the wings and forward fuselage section. The work will be shared among Mitsubishi Heavy Industries (MHI), Fuji Heavy Industries (FHI) and Kawasaki Heavy Industries (KHI). MHI will be responsible for the wing box. KHI will provide the remaining part of the forward fuselage, the main landing gear wheel well and the main wing fixed trailing edge. FHI covers the centre wing box and the integration of this module with the main landing gear wheel well. Vought Aircraft Industries and Alenia Aeronautica of Italy will supply the horizontal tail plane and the centre and aft fuselage sections, which in total will account for around 26 per cent of the 7E7 structure. Boeing itself will supply approximately 35 per cent of the structure including the vertical fin, the fixed and movable leading edges of the wings, the flight deck and part of the forward fuselage section. Final assembly of the 7E7 will take place at Boeing's main plant at Everett in the state of Washington.
- *Airbus A380*. Engine suppliers are Rolls-Royce and Engine Alliance. The work share on the main structural sections of the A380 has been divided mainly between Airbus' production sites in France, Germany, the United Kingdom and Spain: Airbus UK produces the wing; Airbus Spain supplies the horizontal tail plane; Airbus Germany produces the front and rear fuselage sections and vertical

United Technologies of which:	USA	34.6	31.0	2,337	1,027	203
Pratt & Whitney		6.6	7.5	–	–	–
GE of which:	USA	575.2	131.7	14,100	2,656	315
GE Engine		10.8	11.4	–	–	
Snecma	France	–	7.27	206	1,267[c]	22
Subsystems (electronic, landing, electrical/hydraulic systems)						
Honeywell	USA	29.3	23.1	1,324	751[d]	108
Goodrich	USA	5.9	4.4	100	312[e]	20
Smiths	UK	4.8	4.9	180		31
Snecma	France	–	7.27	206	1,267[c]	22
Parker Hannifin	USA	–	6.4	196	122	46
Rockwell Collins	USA	2.6	2.5	258	216	14
Interiors						
B/E Aerospace	USA	1.1	0.62	– 54	0.19	3
Zodiac	France	–	1.66	130	–	10
JAMCO	Japan	247	0.29	3	11.4	1.5
Materials (aluminium and titanium)						
Alcoa	USA	31.7	21.5	936	194	120
Alcan	Canada	32.0	13.7	160	140	88

Sources: Company reports; Mergent; OSIRIS.
Notes: [a] Company reported as self-funded; [b] Company reported, of which US$ 229 million were customer sponsored; [c] Company reported, of which US$ 705 million were self-financed; [d] Company reported, an additional US$ 608 million for R&D in 2003 funded by customers, principally the US government; [e] Company reported, of which US$ 88.4 million are from customers.

form the core of the world's aerospace industry for the coming decades, there is hardly a single supplier at any level in the supply chain from indigenous firms in developing countries. Once the suppliers have been fixed for the respective aircraft, it is extremely difficult for new entrants to displace the established suppliers. A strong 'lock-in' effect operates with 'aligned suppliers' that have developed technologies to meet the specific needs of the systems integrator. They may have a sophisticated understanding of the direction that is needed in technical progress in order to meet the customer's needs. They may also have the benefit of economies of scale achieved over years of supplying a specific programme and have developed invaluable experience in producing the given product over time. They may have developed a relationship of trust with the customer over the long term. In sum, it will be extremely difficult for indigenous firms in developing countries to enter the supply chain of the world's leading systems integrators and compete successfully on the 'global level playing field' with the established members of the supply chain. Consolidation has affected every level of the industry, with even small 'niches' occupies by a small number of focused, technically sophisticated firms.

4
The Beverage Industry

It might be expected that the beverage industry had a low level of global industrial concentration. There has been little apparent long-term change in the nature of its core products, such as beer and carbonated soft drinks. One of the world's fastest-growing beverage markets is in bottled water, the simplest of all consumer products. The sector has negligible investment in research and development. The industry has relatively low entry barriers. In today's high-income countries there used to be a highly fragmented industrial structure, with thousands of firms in each of these sectors in most large countries. However, this industry has experienced intensive industrial consolidation through mergers and acquisitions during the past two decades. In addition, these structural changes have affected the entire global beverage value chain through systems integration by the world's leading beverage companies.

4.1   Consolidation of system integrators

Powerful economies of scale, especially in procurement and branding, have stimulated the process of global consolidation that has swept across the beverage industry in both soft drinks and beer.[17]

Procurement of material inputs

Although the industry does not directly spend significantly on research and development, it spends large amounts procuring material inputs, which directly, or indirectly, use advanced technologies. The world's leading beverage firms spend several billions of dollars each on procurement of material inputs each year. There are large advantages of scale in procurement for the giant global firms. These companies have increasingly moved towards centralizing the procurement of material inputs at a national, regional and, even, a global level. This provides increased leverage over suppliers, enabling them to reduce costs per unit and obtain better terms of supply than their smaller rivals. Non-price advantages deriving from scale include close interaction with their supply chain to ensure that technical progress is oriented towards their particular requirements, and mutual planning of investment, including plant location, around the world.

Branding

A key competitive advantage of the world's leading beverage companies is their ability to construct powerful brands. These are often on a global scale, such as Coca-Cola, Fanta, Sprite, PepsiCo, Budweiser, Heineken, Carlsberg, and Stella Artois. As well as building powerful global brands, the world's leading beverage firms have acquired large portfolios of local brands through merger and acquisition. Building powerful global and regional brands requires large and effectively organized marketing expenditure. In 2003, worldwide expenditure on advertising totalled around US$ 326 billion, with large additional expenditure on other forms of marketing (Sorrell, 2005).[18] The world's leading beverage and food companies spend several billions of dollars each on marketing.[19] The world's leading beverage producers are able to use their large expenditures on marketing to leverage better terms with the marketing agencies.

By 2002, the leading sectors of the beverage industry were highly concentrated globally, with a small number of giant firms, all headquartered in the high-income countries, at the centre of their respective industries (see Table 4.1). In the soft drinks industry, the world's top five firms account for over one-half of all global beverage sales (see Table 4.2).

Table 4.1   The world's leading beverage companies, by sales revenue (US$ billion, 2002: beverage sales only)

Soft drinks		Beer	
Coca-Cola (USA)	75.7	Anheuser-Busch (USA)	13.6
PepsiCo (USA)	41.2	Heineken (EU)	10.8
Danone (EU)	15.5	Kirin (Japan)	9.6
Nestlé (EU)	12.9	SABMiller (EU)	8.3
Cadbury Schweppes (EU)	10.0	Interbrew (EU)	7.3

Source: Euromonitor.

Table 4.2   Global market share of leading soft drinks firms, 2002 (%)

	Soft drinks market share
Coca-Cola	24.5
PepsiCo	13.3
Danone	5.0
Nestlé	4.2
Cadbury Schweppes	3.2
Sub-total	50.2

Source: Euromonitor.

Table 4.3   Coca-Cola and PepsiCo in the global CSD industry, 1999

Country	Coca-Cola's share	PepsiCo's share	Country	Coca-Cola's share	PepsiCo's share
Europe (%)			**Asia-Pacific (%)**		
Germany	56	8	China	34	16
UK	43	12	Philippines	70	18
Spain	60	16	Japan	55	11
Italy	45	8	Australia	57	10
France	60	8	Thailand	52	45
Russia	26	12	India	56	44
Poland	28	17	South Korea	54	13
Netherlands	45	15	Indonesia	94	6
Hungary	57	29	Pakistan	25	71
Romania	44	9	Vietnam	63	36
The Americas (%)			**Africa and Middle East (%)**		
USA	44	31	South Africa	97	0
Canada	39	35	Saudi Arabia	24	76
Mexico	70	19	Egypt	60	40
Brazil	51	7	Israel	70	14
Argentina	59	24	Morocco	96	4
Colombia	60	8			
Venezuela	70	30			
Chile	81	4			
Peru	50	16	Total world	53%	21%

Source: Yoffie (2004).

In the carbonated soft drinks (CSDs) sector, the level of industry concentration is particularly high, as the top two firms, Coca-Cola and PepsiCo, accounted for over 70 per cent of total global sales in 2002. In the United States, the world's largest beverage market, the level of concentration has increased dramatically, with the combined share of the two largest concentrate manufacturers, Coca-Cola and PepsiCo, increasing from 54 per cent in 1966 to 64 per cent in 1980 and 76 per cent in 2000.[20] If one includes Cadbury Schweppes, the top three concentrate manufacturers accounted for over 90 per cent of the US$ 60 billion carbonated soft drink market in the United States at the end of the twentieth century. Over the past two decades, the American beverage giants have been able to achieve a similar level of domination across the world's major beverage markets. In 1999, Coca-Cola and PepsiCo were estimated to account for 74 per cent of all CSD beverages sold worldwide. In almost every country, the two cola giants have managed to achieve a combined share of over 50 per cent (see Table 4.3).

The beer industry is somewhat less concentrated than the soft drinks industry, despite the accelerating pace of mergers and acquisitions in recent years. The top three firms in the United States account for 79 per cent of the total market, while in Japan and most leading European markets, the top two or three firms account for over 70 per cent of the total market (see Table 4.4). Moreover, the leading firms such as Anheuser-Busch, Interbrew, SABMiller, Heineken, and S&N, all have strong positions in more than one major international market.

Table 4.4 Market share of leading beer companies in selected countries, 2002

	Market share (%)		Market share (%)
USA		Italy	
Anheuser-Busch	49	Heineken	35
SABMiller	19	SABMiller	25
Coors	11	Japan	
France		Asahi	38
S&N	40	Kirin	36
Heineken	34	UK	
Interbrew	12	S&N	27
Germany		Interbrew	17
Interbrew	12	Carlsberg	10
Holsten	11	Coors	16
Rackberger	10		
Heineken	8		

Sources: Company annual reports; Company websites; Euromonitor.

4.2 Systems integration: a case study of the Coca-Cola value chain

The world's leading beverage companies stand at the apex of a long supply chain. They relentlessly drive down costs across the whole supply chain, acting as 'systems integrators' so that they can provide low-cost, high-quality products in a highly competitive marketplace. In this chapter, we take a close look at systems integration efforts by The Coca-Cola Company (TCCC), the world's largest beverage company. TCCC sells soft drink beverages in more than 200 countries worldwide; over 70 per cent of its revenues is generated from markets outside of North America. In 2003, the company generated US$ 21 billion mostly from concentrate sales and commanded a market capitalization of over US$ 100 billion, while the respective figures for *the Coca-Cola system*, which refers to TCCC and its bottlers, are many times larger.

4.2.1 The Coca-Cola value chain

Since 1923, TCCC has operated under a franchise model in which the company manufactures and sells concentrate to its bottlers, each of whom then has the right to manufacture and distribute Coca-Cola products in a region as specified in the franchise contract. Over the twentieth century, the franchise model has allowed TCCC to grow rapidly while realizing economies of scale and scope in branding and marketing, procurement, concentrate manufacturing, and bottling. The Coca-Cola system has grown to immense scale. At the end of the twentieth century, TCCC's bottling system involved many hundreds of bottling plants across the world and over 650,000 employees. If the Coca-Cola system were to be considered as one single firm, it would exceed the size of the largest global industrial companies such as General Motors, Ford and GE in terms of total employment. In terms of value, the Coca-Cola system worldwide is estimated to command sales of over US$ 86 billion, four times as large as the Coca-Cola Company, and would have ranked number 20 on the *Global 500* (versus the Coca-Cola Company itself at number 237), behind IBM but ahead of Siemens.[21]

A simple Coca-Cola product requires a wide array of purchased inputs of goods and services. Surrounding the Coca-Cola system is a massive supply chain, the functions of which are deeply influenced by Coca-Cola's company activities. The most visible part of the whole Coca-Cola value chain is the franchised bottlers that manufacture the final product, but beyond this is a huge 'extended firm', each component of which contributes to the final product. It includes the manufacturers of primary packaging, the can makers, the PET makers, and the glass bottle makers; the machinery makers whose products are used to fill the primary packaging and the transport equipment makers that distribute the finished product (and sometimes transport primary packaging back to the bottlers for refilling); the machinery makers whose machines produce the inputs for primary packaging, such as 'pre-forms' and 'blowing machines'; the manufacturers of primary materials from which the primary packaging is made, such as the makers of 'bottle-grade resin', and the makers of specialized, high-technology steel and aluminium for metal cans. The value chain also includes the huge number of workers in the sugar industry, who grow and process sugar, as well as the farm workers and factory employees who process fruit into concentrate. Throughout the value chain there is a large system of logistics that transports Coca-Cola inputs and final products. Selling Coca-Cola products requires heavy involvement of the marketing industry. Finally, Coca-Cola products reach the final customers through a massive retail system, involving a vast network of small 'mom-and-pop' stores, restaurants and other final sales points, as well as a fast-growing network of 'modern trade', including quick-service restaurants, cinema chains, petrol stations, and, of course, the rapidly growing network of modern retailers, including convenience stores, supermarkets and hypermarkets.

One way of visualizing this complex web of business relationships in the Coca-Cola value chain is to conceive of The Coca-Cola Company as embedded in a set of 'concentric rings' of business relationships. The Coca-Cola Company is at the heart of the entire structure. The first 'concentric ring' consists of the licenced bottlers, or the so-called franchise bottlers. It is the Coca-Cola Company and its franchise bottlers together that the company itself terms the 'Coca-Cola system' (Nolan, 1999). Outer 'concentric rings' consist of the direct suppliers of goods and services to the Coca-Cola system. This consists of firms supplying inputs directly used by the Coca-Cola system, such as marketing equipment, bottling lines, transport equipment, cans, bottles and sugar; and the suppliers of goods and services including such products as raw sugar, aluminium, tinplate, and PET pre-form blowing machines. The entire supply chain, working to meet the expanding needs of the Coca-Cola system, can be regarded as the 'external firm' (ibid.).

Coca-Cola sits at the centre of this immense structure, monitoring the performance of the whole value chain, stimulating institutional change, pushing relentlessly for cost reduction, promoting technical progress, and improving product quality, in order to compete with its main international competitor, PepsiCo, as well as leading East Asian and global beverage companies. As global competition has intensified, Coca-Cola's competitive advantages have become critically dependent upon its ability to nurture and orchestrate its value chain to push the Coca-Cola product 'within an arm's reach of desire' of mass consumers across the world.

From its earliest days, TCCC had thought about 'knitting together' the value chain, as noted in its 1922 *Annual Report*:

> Coca-Cola's true place in industry cannot be appreciated without knowledge of its manufacturing distribution and sales facilities: Fourteen regional factories. Ten divisional warehouses. Twelve hundred bottlers. Two thousand jobbers. One hundred and five thousand fountain dealers. One hundred and fifty thousand bottle dealers. These are knitted together into an organization with the purpose of joining the selling force of all into a single selling force behind every ounce of Coca-Cola that is manufactured (Coca-Cola, *Annual Report, 1922*: 19).

The nature of the concentric rings in the value chain has altered drastically over time. As the company grew, in particular in the past few decades, the concentric rings became spatially wider. They have become truly global in the past two decades or so. Certain activities have been sometimes included in the core and at other times shifted to outer rings. However, throughout, there has been a fundamental continuity in the intermeshing of the company with the surrounding business systems, extending right across the value chain. The competitive success of the Coca-Coca Company has relied heavily upon managing well the relationships among the interests of different parts of the concentric rings (Nolan, 1999).

Nolan (1999) observed that the function of TCCC within the business system has changed sharply since the 1970s to become 'more cerebral', with a large proportion of its employees engaged in complex brainwork. Indeed, a substantial portion of TCCC's activities has been undertaken to plan, coordinate and sometimes reshape the surrounding business system according to its long term strategic needs. TCCC's ability to integrate the most important parts of its value chain stems mainly from the power of the Coca-Cola brand and the enormous procurement spending by the Coca-Cola system.

The Coca-Cola brand is arguably the most important asset in the Coca-Cola system. For the *consumer*, the Coca-Cola brand creates value by associating the beverage with images of freshness, excitement, fun and youth. More importantly, the Coca-Cola brand is also perceived by consumers across the world to be associated with the American ideals of freedom and development.[22] By purchasing the product, consumers are therefore buying a piece of lifestyle that is distinctively American. For *retailers*, the Coca-Cola brand, with its instant consumer recognition, generates faster stock turnovers, greater sales and higher returns on assets. For *bottlers and suppliers*, the Coca-Cola brand provides the central glue that 'knits together' the different parts of the Coca-Cola system. The brand induces participants to invest in the business system because it signifies market power, consumer acceptance, financial strength and therefore good economics (Nolan, 1999). At the same time, the brand places intense demands on all related firms to provide high quality services, consistent with its high quality image. For TCCC, the Coca-Cola brand not only creates value for the whole business system, but also ensures that the company captures a relatively large portion of the value created. TCCC's investment in brand building includes advertising, sponsorships and special promotional events. Between 1998 and 2003, TCCC's cumulative spending on global advertising alone was over US$ 10 billion. In addition, TCCC has also invested substantially in the sales promotion of its beverages. Retailers and distributors receive rebates, promotions and point-of-sale displays. Bottling partners receive advertising support and funds designated for cold drink equipment. Consumers receive coupons, discounts and promotional incentives. In 2003 alone, TCCC spent approximately US$ 3.7 billion in these promotion programmes. Today, the Coca-Cola brand has become one of the most potent symbols of American culture, contributing to the significant homogenization of social and cultural values across the world. In 2003, Coca-Cola was ranked by Interbrand as the most powerful global brand with a total value of US$ 70 billion.[23]

In the late 1990s, the global Coca-Cola bottling system spent over US$ 15 billion annually on the procurement of packaging, ingredients, marketing equipment, transport equipment, new plant and production lines.[24] This enormous spending power has allowed The Coca-Cola Company to shape the structure of its value chain. In the late 1990s, TCCC established Global Procurement and Trading (GP&T) to coordinate and consolidate input procurement across the global Coca-Cola system. Through GP&T, TCCC has not only substantially lowered procurement costs across the value chain but also selectively established long-term strategic relationships with key suppliers, which have planned their global expansion with that of the Coca-Cola system.

Through these strategic relationships, TCCC achieves input consistency and lower procurement cost, while its strategic suppliers benefit from economies of scale in supplying the Coca-Cola system globally. In order to maintain the high quality image of the Coca-Cola brand, an important aspect of Coca-Cola's relationship with its suppliers is the stringent quality control of every aspect associated with the production and distribution of the final product. All suppliers for the Coca-Cola system have to be approved directly by Coca-Cola's technical department after thorough assessment of product quality, production and quality assurance processes. In addition, the close relationship with suppliers allows TCCC to continuously drive innovation in the value chain that serves its strategic needs.

4.2.2   Coca-Cola and its bottlers

Coca-Cola's integrative function is perhaps most apparent in its role in the restructuring of the bottling system. The bottlers have always played a key role in connecting TCCC with a wide array of business activities in the value chain. The balancing of the interest of the first and the outer tiers against each other is also at the heart of the Coca-Cola system. The fact that the company has used the franchise system as its basic method of operation for over a century has made it acutely sensitive to the need for mutuality of interest and a long-term perspective between the core and the surrounding businesses.[25] This relationship has been described as one of 'simultaneous dependence and interdependence' (Neville Isdell, Chief Executive Officer, Coca-Cola Beverages, interview). To meet the changing nature of the business competition, both in the United States and globally, the franchise bottling system of TCCC experienced substantial changes.

The first franchises to bottle Coca-Cola were issued in the United States in the mid-1890s. The initial franchises were for a very small territory, limited by the distance that a horse-drawn vehicle could cover in a single day. Consequently, there were hundreds of franchises within the United States. In 1956, there was a total of 1,694 bottlers globally, of which 1,100 were within the United States and Canada, and 594 outside (Coca-Cola, *Annual Report, 1956*: 13). From the 1950s through to the 1980s, there occurred a substantial consolidation of bottlers. A 'minor consolidation' took place after the Second World War, followed by a 'dramatic consolidation' in the 1960s and the 1970s. It was driven partly by mergers initiated by the bottlers in response to changing technology in filling plants, especially the rise of high-output canning plants, which required more capital than small, regional glass bottle plants. It was affected also by growth of customer consolidation. Larger customers required unified packaging and centralized negotiation of deliveries. The consolidation was strongly supported by the company headquarters in Atlanta.

The decades since 1980 have been the phase of the most explosive growth in the history of the Coca-Cola Company. In this period it has become a truly global firm. Continuation with the old system of small, independently owned bottlers would have led to an explosion in the number of bottlers, which would have led to large problems of system control, and almost certainly, powerful managerial diseconomies of scale. It would have become increasingly difficult to maintain alignment of interest among the different actors in the global system. Moreover, system growth itself required consolidation of bottlers. The small size of the average bottler would have presented difficulties in generating capital to invest in larger, least-cost plants. The rate of expansion would have been further slowed by the fact that the system as a whole would have been higher cost and less competitive.

The surrounding economic system within which the Coca-Cola system operated was itself changing at high speed, including a strong move towards consolidation of customers: 'around the world, our customers are growing larger, consolidating and crossing national borders with increasing frequency, particularly within the fast changing European Community' (Coca-Cola, *Annual Report*, *1989*: 7). Dealing with fast growing customers required very different managerial skills from those of the traditional small-scale local bottler: 'in addition to serving small, purely local customers, our bottlers must now command the resources necessary to serve the licensees and local division of global enterprises' (Coca-Cola, *Annual Report*, *1989*: 7). In other words, globalization was stimulating further globalization. Globalization by companies in different, but related sectors within the value chain was forcing other companies within the value chain to globalize also (Nolan, 1999).

Since the early 1980s, the massive Coca-Cola bottling system has gone through a revolution. Instead of a proliferation in the number of bottlers, there has been a dramatic reduction in their number. The company's headquarters has guided this process carefully. It has constituted a complex exercise in corporate planning and may be thought of as the exercise of a 'visible hand' reorganizing a large swathe of the soft drinks industry. The first 'anchor bottler', Coca-Cola Enterprises (CCE), was founded in 1985.[26] Within ten years, the anchor bottlers already accounted for around 38 per cent of worldwide unit case volume

(Coca-Cola, *Annual Report, 1998*: 34) and over 45 per cent of the Coca-Cola system's worldwide sales (Morgan Stanley, 1998: 110). Their share rose rapidly as consolidation of bottlers proceeded rapidly in the mid-1990s (see below). The share of independently owned bottlers had fallen to just 40 per cent of global Coca-Cola sales (Coca-Cola, *Annual Report, 1996*: 39). In the process of restructuring each of the anchor bottlers is en route to becoming a large multi-plant, multinational company. These include CCE, Coca-Cola Amatil (CCA), Swire (based in Hong Kong), CCEAG (formed in 1996 in Germany), Coca-Cola Femsa SA (operating in Argentina and Mexico), Panamerican Beverages (designated an anchor bottler in 1995), Coca-Cola Nordic Beverages and Coca-Cola Sabco (South and East Africa). Coca-Cola Beverages joined them in July 1998 as it demerged from CCA.

By 1991, the company had invested in ownership shares in bottlers accounting for 38 per cent of the total amount of Coca-Cola sold worldwide (Coca-Cola, *Annual Report, 1991*: 37). In most situations where Coca-Cola took an equity position, it used this position 'to secure capable, aggressive executives to manage these operations' (Coca-Cola, *Annual Report, 1990*: 8). This was typically followed by rapid growth of per capita sales and sharply improved performance of the companies concerned. This was a new epoch in which the company headquarters became highly active in restructuring the whole Coca-Cola system, with the bottlers at the core.

The restructuring of the bottling system over the past two decades has led to a profound shift in the relationship between The Coca-Cola Company and the bottling system. While this is an important phenomenon in its own right, the process of explosive concentration of bottlers has large consequential effects upon the relationship of the first and second tier with the third and fourth tier supplier firms. The successful accomplishment of these changes laid a foundation for the company's explosive growth of sales and profitability in the late 1980s and the 1990s. It is an important episode in the business history concerning the epoch of globalization.

4.2.3   Coca-Cola and the global consumer packaging industry

A major part of TCCC's competitive advantage is embedded in the nature of its packaging, which is an integral part of the company's cost structure and marketing strategy. Coca-Cola's power to shape the industry structure and set the pace of technological progress in the global consumer packaging industry came from its enormous purchasing clout. The Coca-Cola system accounts for a large fraction of the total global use of packaging, increasing quantities of which are recycled. It is estimated to purchase close to 30 per cent of the total global production of cans of all kinds, including all uses, from dog food to canned fruit. It accounts for almost one half of the total use of cans by the world's soft drinks industry. The Coca-Cola system buys around one-quarter of the world total of milled aluminium plate. It accounts for 5 per cent of the world's consumption of PET and roughly half of that consumed by the world's soft drinks industry. It accounts for around 5 per cent of global consumption of glass for containers, and close to 40 per cent of that used by the world's soft drinks industry. In 1997, within the EU alone, the Coca-Cola system spent US$ 1.4 billion on the major items of packaging (Nolan, 1998).

Within each product category, the company has relentlessly attempted to drive down costs of production, while enhancing quality and functionality. It has worked closely with the first and second tier suppliers to achieve advances in packaging technology. These work to drive down costs for the bottlers, enabling the whole Coca-Cola system to provide low-cost, high-quality products in a highly competitive marketplace. A major goal of Coca-Cola's technology drive has been weight reduction, driven by the need to reduce costs of production and compete in the market place. In each of the main areas of primary packaging, that is, glass, metal and PET, Coca-Cola has taken the lead in pushing suppliers to 'lightweight' their products.

Packaging innovations were not just designed to reduce the cost of the container. Many important innovations were intended mainly to increase sales by improving convenience for different use occasions. The introduction of the ring pull on metal cans in the mid-1960s had a huge and largely unanticipated impact on sales. The development of plastic technology that enabled the contour PET bottle also had increased sales as its major goal, leveraging a key aspect of the Coca-Cola image, the 'contour' bottle design. The introduction of the 20-oz (600 ml) PET bottle in 1994 had a huge impact on sales. This helped justify the product's 'premium' brand positioning, as opposed to the 'industrial' image of the straight-wall can and PET bottle. Other innovations were designed to improve the shelf life and guarantee the quality of the product for the consumer. For example, the development in metal can technology meant that fresh cold drinks retained their fizz and flavour almost indefinitely, in 'a pack whose design is almost as demanding as an aircraft's wing' (*FT*, 10 December 1997). Improvements in closure technology had a similar impact on product quality and shelf life in plastic and glass bottles.

Innovations designed with one end in view sometimes also produced cost savings in other areas. For example, delivery schedules were simplified by the fact that the improved quality of metal cans meant that product could be kept longer without deterioration. Moreover, there are large externalities involved in the relentless long-run drive to light-weighting. The fall in metal consumption per unit of primary packaging tended to reduce the rate of depletion of exhaustible resources, attributable to consumption of packaging. The dramatic fall in weight meant that fuel consumption for the delivery of given volumes of product was reduced. The reduction in the amount of raw material input used has had a significant effect on the rate of depletion of bauxite and iron ore:

'The drive for cost reductions from the leading drinks companies – Coca-Cola used almost 30 per cent of the 190 billion cans made [in 1996] – has cut the weight of the average aluminium can by one third from 18 gm to less than 11 gm. This may not sound much, but it means that US industry, for instance, has saved more than 6 million tons of aluminium in the past three decades.' (*FT*, 10 December 1997)

Stimulating and leading changes in packaging has been a central part of the construction and development of Coca-Cola's brand identity. It has worked to stimulate suppliers to develop technologies that enhance the distinctive imagery of Coca-Cola products, such as the ring-pull, narrow-necking, the one-piece metal can and the early straight wall PET bottle, progressing in recent years to the contour plastic bottle, and most recently, to the contour metal can.[27]

In many of the key technical advances in soft drinks packaging, Coca-Cola has been responsible for setting the design goal and often for advancing part of the development costs of the new product. It has often led the industry in stimulating sales-enhancing packaging innovations, which have in time become the standard industry packages. In recent years, the pace of change has accelerated, with a sequence of important changes in packaging initiated with the introduction of cans as long ago as 1960. Part of the process of transformation in packaging involves competition between different materials, including steel, aluminium, glass and plastics. The pace of technical change in each of these areas is rapid.

Coca-Cola and the global beverage can industry

Coca-Cola is the world's largest purchaser of beverage cans: it used almost 30 per cent of the 190 billion cans made in 1996 (*FT*, 10 December

1997). It has had a deep influence on the whole development of the industry. The early development of the metal can for use in the beverage industry took place independently of the company. However, the company relentlessly pushed for 'light-weighting' in order to drive down costs of production, including raw material, power and water consumed to make the cans, and transport costs which are reduced by lighter cans. When the first 12-oz (355 ml) metal beverage can was introduced in 1961 it weighed 164 lbs per 1,000 units. Coca-Cola made clear its wish to be able to purchase lightweight cans, which reduced costs across the Coca-Cola system by saving on both raw material consumption and transport costs per can. Lighter cans also were more appealing to consumers.

The steel industry responded by a new technology called double cold reduction that reduced the weight of steel for metal cans by around one-third. The new technology enabled substantial reductions in the amount of steel required per can. At this stage the can still bore the cost and technical disadvantages of a soldered side seam. The company urged the suppliers to eliminate the side seam altogether. Continental Can developed a welded side seam. American Can developed an adhesive bonded side seam, and the solder was eliminated. This in turn eliminated the need for the tin coating. The aluminium industry competed for a share of the 12-oz beverage can market and developed the two-piece aluminium can. The steel industry responded with the development of the two-piece steel can.

The two industries, steel and aluminium, continued to innovate and further reduce the weight of the beverage can by metallurgical innovations, design changes and process improvements. Some of the advances are embodied in the shape of the packaging container. Important among these was the development of the 'necked-in' can, which resulted in substantial savings of metal per can, since the heaviest concentration of metal is in the lid. By the 1990s, the weight of the 12-oz aluminium beverage can had fallen to just 35 lbs. per 1,000 units, a decline in weight of 41 per cent compared to the first aluminium cans. The 12-oz metal can now weighed just one-fifth of the first beverage cans used by Coca-Cola in the early 1960s. Progressively thinner walls for cans reduced the amount of steel or aluminium needed per package, drastically lowering material input costs per can. This in turn reduced the energy needed to produce soft drink packages, which further reduced unit costs for can manufacturers. Also, the necked-in can is easier to crush, reducing the energy costs involved in recycling metal cans.

The Coca-Cola Company has a strong interest in the emergence of globally powerful large-scale purchasing suppliers that can make the massive capital investment in a network of global plants, undertake the requisite R&D and bargain with their own supply chain. However, Coca-Cola also has an interest in ensuring that there is intense competition among its global suppliers. In this sense, TCCC acts as a form of internal competition authority to help shape the structure of its supply chain.

Coca-Cola and the global PET industry

The Coca-Cola Company played an important role in stimulating the use of PET to manufacture beverage bottles. A major factor in leading Coca-Cola to push for the development of plastic bottles to replace and/or supplement glass bottles was the research it sponsored into the environmental impact of the different materials. Following many years of research, in 1970 the company commissioned one of the first environmental impact studies for a set of consumer products. The results of the research were to many people counter-intuitive. Because of the large amount of energy per unit of product in the production of glass and in transporting such a heavy package, Coca-Cola found that in certain circumstances the energy intensity involved in the life cycle of the plastic bottle was less than that of the glass bottle. This gave it the confidence to proceed with the development of the plastic bottle. The successful development of this product, which began as early as 1968, was to have large externalities for the whole soft drink industry, in which the product has now become a standard form of packaging.

The assurance of a large potential demand from Coca-Cola's bottling system stimulated the early development of this technology, reducing the risk associated with the necessary investment. Coca-Cola worked closely with leading PET makers, such as Continental Plastics in Europe, as well as working directly with resin manufacturers such as DuPont, ICI and Hoechst, to push forwards the technology of PET bottles. PET technology has advanced steadily. Packaging became stronger and less liable to breakage. It enabled the product to have a longer storage life without product deterioration. PET bottles also became steadily lighter, thus reducing energy costs per unit manufactured and transported. Important developments stimulated by Coca-Cola were the removal of the heavy base cup on large-sized PET bottles. Walls became steadily thinner. New shapes allowed the use of more efficient packing methods. Stronger forms of PET enabled multiple reuse of washable, refillable bottles. The company worked closely with a leading PET maker to produce the first refillable PET bottle technology. Coca-Cola also worked closely with another company, Hoechst Celanese, to produce the first PET bottle with recycled content. In the 1990s, the company pioneered the 'sandwich' method, which encloses recycled material between layers of virgin plastic.

4.3   Cascade effect in the beverage value chain

The effect of the systems integration efforts by the world leading beverage companies, such as Coca-Cola, on material inputs and services has been to increase the pressure for consolidation from the higher reaches of the supply chain. The closely related food industry has undergone its own process of consolidation, resulting in the emergence of a group of super-large firms (see Table 4.5). In many areas, the 'cascade' effect pressures on the supply chain from the beverage industry are applied simultaneously by the food industry.

This 'cascade effect' has stimulated a wave of consolidation in the respective parts of the supply chain. Moreover, as the higher reaches of the supply chain have struggled to meet the global needs of the world's leading beverage companies, the process of consolidation within their ranks has produced further 'cascade' pressure on the supply chain of

Table 4.5   The world's leading food companies, 2003

Company name	Revenues (US$ bn)	Assets (US$ bn)	Profits (US$ bn)	Profits/ revenues (%)	Employees (000s)
Nestlé	65.4	72.4	4.62	7.1	253
Cargill	60.0	–	–	–	–
Unilever	48.3	47.9	3.13	6.5	234
Archer Daniels Midland	30.7	17.2	0.45	1.5	26
PepsiCo	27.0	25.3	3.57	13.2	143
Tyson Foods	24.5	10.5	0.34	1.3	120
Bunge	22.3	9.9	0.41	1.8	23
Conagro Foods	22.1	15.1	0.78	3.5	63
Coca-Cola	21.0	27.3	4.35	20.1	49
Sara Lee	18.3	15.1	1.22	6.7	146
Groupe Danone	16.4	21.3	0.15	0.9	89
Anheuser-Busch	14.1	14.7	2.08	14.8	23
Diageo	11.5	26.7	0.12	1.0	36
COFCO	13.3	5.5	0.11	0.8	25

Source: *Fortune*, 26 July 2004.

these firms, as they struggle to lower costs, and achieve the technical progress necessary to meet the fierce demands of the world's leading system integrators who stand at the centre of their respective supply chains.

4.3.1   Global consumer goods packaging

The global consumer packaging industry is a huge industry, worth about US$ 300 billion annually. It is growing at around 4 per cent annually, with the fastest growth rate being recorded in China and Latin America. The food and beverage sectors account for about 65 per cent of global packaging consumption (49 per cent for food and 15 per cent for beverages). Plastic (PET) packaging has become the largest packaging type, accounting for 40 per cent of the total, and is growing at a much faster rate than the other types. The fast growth of this segment is attributable to its convenience and its advantageous material properties such as lightweight and transparency. Metal containers account for one-fifth of the global total. The share of glass packaging has been shrinking, and now stands at only one-tenth of the total. However, glass has created growth opportunities through lightweight and other special features such as decorated containers with a high appeal for consumers of 'premium' businesses. It is still experiencing significant positive demand growth of around one per cent per annum globally, despite its falling share in the total packaging industry. Metal containers have witnessed a stronger performance than glass, owing to the increases in consumption of packaged soft drinks and beer. Paper-based packaging still accounts for three-tenths of the global total, and is still an important part of secondary packaging in the beverage industry.

   Growth of packaging expenditure tends to be quite closely correlated with growth of national product per capita. In addition, changes in lifestyle, demographic structure and consumer preference also has affected the industry. Convenience has become a central driver in packaging innovation, especially as the younger generation across the world tends to have a busier lifestyle and prefers to live in smaller household units. The combination of factors affecting packaging preferences is somewhat different in different product types. For example, in beer, the changing pattern of consumption from draught beer to packaged premium beers has stimulated tremendous growth of metal and plastic packaging. In CSDs, consumers' preference for light weight and ease of chilling, and producers' preference for lower transport costs has allowed plastic bottles to gradually substitute for glass bottles, while metal cans have just managed to maintain their share.

The world's leading beverage firms interact closely with the leaders of the packaging industry to work together for ways to meet their needs better through innovations in product and process technologies. Technical progress has also been achieved through contributions from the primary material suppliers in the aluminium, steel, PET resin industries, as well as in the suppliers of machinery. The world's leading beverage firms have interacted with this process at every step, acting as 'systems integrators' for the overall process of technical progress.

A major goal of the system integrators' technology drive has been weight reduction, driven by the need to reduce costs of production across the whole supply chain. In each of the main areas of primary packaging, glass, metal and PET (plastic), the world's leading beverage firms have taken the lead in pushing suppliers to 'lightweight' their products. Other packaging goals for the leading beverage companies include improved safety, attractiveness of appearance, longer product life, and ease of handling.

There is still great uncertainty about the way materials used in the soft drink container industry will progress. In both the soft drinks and the beer industry, the glass bottle was the sole form of primary packaging until the 1960s. In both parts of the industry, the metal can came to account for close to half of all primary packaging. However, this was followed by the rise of PET plastic, which has overtaken the metal can in the soft drinks industry, pushing the glass bottle into third position. However, in the beer sector, the glass bottle remains as important as the metal can in most markets, with only slow progress of the PET bottle. The three different forms of primary packaging compete intensively with each other for market share, pushing forward technical progress constantly in the search for packaging that is safe; which is of high quality (keeping the product in good condition longer); which can be recycled; which is attractive in appearance; and, above all, which is of lighter weight.

All sectors of the packaging industry, including plastic, metal and glass containers, caps and closures, paperboard and labels, have experienced rapid consolidation in recent years. The top ten global packaging firms account for between 40 and 80 per cent of global markets, depending on the sector.

Metal cans

The metal can segment of the packaging industry has experienced high-speed growth since the early 1990s. It is estimated that there are now around 210 billion cans of beer and soft drinks consumed annually.

Table 4.6 Global market share of top ten firms
in different packaging sectors

Packaging sector	Global market share of top ten firms (%)
Rigid plastics	40
Flexible plastics	50
Caps/closures	52
Paperboard	58
Labels	62
Glass containers	75
Metal containers	80

Source: Rexam Consumer Packaging Report 2003: 7.

The world's metal can industry has undergone a process of high-speed consolidation during the epoch of the global business revolution, since the late 1980s. The bulk of the world's metal beverage cans are consumed in North America and Europe, with a total consumption of 144 billion cans in 2003, accounting for almost 70 per cent of total world consumption of beverage cans. Three firms now stand out as the global leaders in this industry: Ball's share of the North American and European market stands at 38 per cent, compared with 27 per cent for Rexam, and 20 per cent for Crown.

Ball
Ball was founded in Buffalo, New York, in 1880, producing tin (steel) cans. By the early 1970s, it was a leader in the beverage can business. Its nine plants in North America produced around 17 billion cans annually.

Table 4.7 Market share of the world's leading beverage can makers in North America and the EU, 2003 (%)

	North America	EU	North America plus EU
Total can consumption (billion cans)	106	38	144
Ball	32	30	31
Rexam	22	42	28
Crown	20	20	20
Metal container	22	–	–

Sources: Ball Corporation (2004); Rexam, US Investor Roadshow Presentation (March 2003).

In the 1990s, it began a period of rapid growth. In 1993, it acquired Heeken Can Company, then the US's largest regional manufacturer of metal food containers. The combination of 11 former Heeken plants with those already owned by Ball made it the third largest producer of metal food and aerosol cans in the North American market. In 1998, it acquired the metal beverage container assets of Reynolds Metals Company, which made Ball the largest supplier of metal beverage cans in North America. In 2002, it acquired the can-making business of Schmalbach-Lubeca AG, a German-based metal beverage company, and renamed its European operations as Ball Packaging Europe.

In 2003, Ball's revenues were US\$ 4.98 billion, with profits of US\$ 230 million. It was ranked number 351 in the US's *Fortune* 500 list (*Fortune*, 14 April 2003). Packaging accounts for around nine-tenths of Ball's total sales. It operates one of the most modern R&D centres in the metal container industry, and has made numerous patented advancements in can and end manufacturing. Some of Ball's technologies have become standards for the whole can industry.

Ball operates around 50 plants, including 20 in North America and 12 in Europe. In 2002, Ball's North American operations still accounted for over two-thirds of the company's total revenue. However, its European operations were greatly increased by the acquisition of Schmalbach-Lubeca's packaging business, which helped to increase Ball's total revenue by 29 per cent in 2003. In 2003, Ball's beverage can sales amounted to US\$ 2.3 billion in North America and US\$ 1.0 billion in Europe. As we have seen, Ball is now the world's largest beverage can maker, accounting for almost two-fifths of the total beverage can output of North America and Europe combined.

Expansion in eastern Europe and Asia forms a core part of Ball's growth strategy. Its international packaging operations include joint ventures in Brazil, China, the Philippines, Taiwan and Thailand and licensees in Australia, Israel, Japan, Mexico, New Zealand and Venezuela.

Crown Holdings

Crown has been a pioneer in packaging technology. In 1892, William Painter, Crown's founder, invented a better way to package soft drinks and beer, patenting the 'crown cork'. Soon thereafter he founded the Crown Cork & Seal Company, in Baltimore. Painter's vision revolutionized the bottling industry. In 1898, Crown Cork introduced automated technology in the shape of the first foot-powered, 'super-crowner'. A good operator could fill and cap 24 bottles per minute, the highest speed at that time. Painter started selling crowning equipment and gained retailers' support for the new bottle-sealing device.

From its earliest days, Crown had an international outlook. The company started its international expansion soon after its establishment because the revolution in bottling spread so quickly. By 1906, when Painter died, Crown had already established operations in Europe, South America and Asia. In order to survive Prohibition, Crown began to shift its production from the beer to the soft drinks industry. During the 1930s, it is estimated that Crown sold around one half of the world's total supply of bottle caps. In 1936, Crown acquired the Acme Can Company of Philadelphia and entered the food can business. In the late 1930s, Crown upgraded the electrolytic tin-plating process and introduced the 'Crowntainer' – a two-piece drawn, 'necked-in' steel can sealed with a crown, which was used as a quart beer can. By the 1960s, Crown had become more strongly focused on the fast-growing soft drinks can business. It started to design and produce products specifically to meet the needs of soft drink companies and it soon gained considerable market share in the US soft drinks market. In 1969, Crown introduced the highly successful two-piece steel beverage can alternative to the aluminium can. In the 1970s, Crown started serious expansion in can making in developing countries. By the end of that decade, Crown had become one of the world's leading producers of cans and crowns and operated 60 plants overseas and its net sales reached US$ 1 billion.

In the 1990s, Crown grew rapidly to establish itself firmly as one of the global leaders in the beverage and food packaging industry. To achieve this it made a series of important acquisitions. In 1990 it acquired major portions of the former industry leader Continental Can Company and became the North American packaging leader. It went into the plastic packaging business in 1992 by acquiring CONSTAR International, a world leader in PET plastic containers for the beverage, food and household markets. In 1996, it greatly strengthened its position in Europe by acquiring Carnaud-Metalbox, which was Europe's leading manufacturer of metal and plastic packaging, and was itself the result of a Franco-British merger. Despite its expansion in plastic packaging, Crown remains mainly focused on metal cans. In 2003, within Crown's total revenues, metal beverage cans and ends accounted for 37 per cent; food cans and can ends accounted for 32 per cent; and other metal packaging accounted for 18 per cent (Crown, *Annual Report, 2003*).

As a result of its vigorous global expansion, Crown's net sales rose up from US$ 1.9 billion in 1989 to over US$ 8 billion by 1997. Crown employs about 28,000 people and operates 190 plants in 44 countries. In 2003, around 70 per cent of Crown's revenues were derived from operations outside of the United States, principally in Europe. The company's key customers are global giants in the beverage and food industries such as Coca-Cola, PepsiCo, Anheuser-Busch, Cadbury Schweppes, Heineken and InBev. Crown regards its long-term relationship with key customers as crucial to its long-term success: its top ten customers account for around 22 per cent of its total sales revenue (Crown, *Annual Report, 2003*: 4).

Crown is proud of its long history of technical innovation in the can industry. In recent years it has spent an average of around US$ 30–40 million per year on R&D, developing both new products and processes that meet the needs of global customers. For example, in the year 2000, Crown introduced the 'SuperEnd™', a revolutionary new can end, arguably the biggest breakthrough in global can technology in two decades. It requires less metal than existing beverage can ends without any reduction in strength. It also offers 'improved appearance, pourability, drinkability and ease-of-opening' (Crown, *Annual Reports*).

Like other leading can makers, Crown regarded its participation in the industry's explosive concentration process as crucial for its survival. However, the period since the late 1990s has been difficult. Crown's net sales actually declined in four successive years, from US$ 7.3 billion in the year 2000 to US$ 6.6 billion in 2003. Even more worryingly for Crown, it experienced losses in each of these years, the worst year being 2001, when it made a loss of US$ 976 million. By 2003, losses had declined to just US$ 32 million (Crown, *Annual Report, 2003*).

Rexam

Rexam was founded in London in 1881 by William Bowater as a firm of paper agents. By the mid-1950s, the group had become the largest newsprint producer in the world. Already in the 1940s, it began to diversify through acquisitions. By the 1980s, it had become a highly diversified conglomerate, with worldwide interests including pulp, papermaking, tissue products, packaging, building materials, builders merchants, furniture, carpet manufacture, freight forwarding, diesel engines, commodities trading, insurance and even merchant banks.

In 1996, Rolf Borjesson took over as chief executive officer, and made a sharp change of strategic direction. The company gradually sold out about 100 business units, leaving consumer packaging as the core business. Borjesson considered that the global expansion of packaging presented enormous opportunities for growth for a focused firm with global reach.

Alongside large-scale divestment of non-core businesses, Borjesson began a process of large-scale mergers and acquisitions. In 1999, Rexam bought PLM, a large Swedish can maker, for US$ 1.1 billion. In 2002, it acquired the American National Can Co. (ANC) for US$ 2.8 billion. At the time of its acquisition by Rexam, ANC was the world's second largest can maker. In 2003, it acquired Latasa, the Brazilian can maker, for US$ 462 million. Following the acquisition, Rexam overtook Ball as the world's largest producer of beverage cans.

When Rexam acquired ANC, Borjesson said: 'We're driven by the consolidation in the market. Our customers are becoming bigger and bigger, and they want fewer and fewer larger suppliers – it makes life easier for them' (quoted in *FT*, 4 April 2002). Rexam's largest customer is Coca-Cola, 'which was closely involved in the deal': 'With the increasing globalization of the industry, the key to steady growth is to become a preferred supplier to multinational customers such as Coca-Cola; . . . [T]he trick is to be one of the selected suppliers, but you can only do that if you have network and the service and logistics' (Borjesson, quoted in *FT*, 4 April 2002).

Rexam's acquisition in October 2003 of South America's leading beverage can maker, Latasa, is highly significant in view of Rexam's stated intention to build its business in South America and China. Latasa is the leading producer and supplier of aluminium beverage cans in Brazil, Argentina and Chile, serving both the brewing and soft drinks industries. In 2002, it had sales of US$ 404 million and an operating profit of US$ 85 million. The acquisition means that Rexam is now the largest can maker in Brazil, one of the world's largest national markets with an annual consumption of approximately 10 billion cans. It will enable Rexam to deepen its relationship with Coca-Cola as well as with InBev, the world's third largest brewer. Rexam will be able to inject its research and development knowledge into Latasa, and to enable it to benefit from economies of scale in procurement, marketing and administration.

Rexam operates about 90 manufacturing plants globally. Its revenues in 2002 totalled £3.2 billion. Beverage packaging now accounts for three-quarters of Rexam's total revenues. Rexam produces different sizes of beverage cans, in both steel and aluminium, and supplies a wide variety of can ends. It employs around 21,000 people worldwide, and is now firmly established as one of the world's top five global packaging companies. In beverage cans, it has an estimated global market share of around 23 per cent (*Business Week*, 26 January 2004).

By 2002, Rexam had become a truly international firm. The United Kingdom, in which Rexam is still headquartered, now accounts for only around 12 per cent of total revenues. Over one third of total revenues are from sales in Continental Europe, and almost one half from the Americas. Rexam views its expansion in Latin America and China as central to its long-term growth strategy (ibid.).

Rexam's revenues grew rapidly after the late 1990s, from £1.9 billion in 1998 to £3.2 billion in 2002 (Rexam, *Annual Reports*), in large part due to the extensive mergers and acquisitions. During most of this period it achieved a reasonable profits performance, with net profits reaching a peak of £158 million in 2001. However, in common with other can makers, Rexam faced a fiercely competitive market, and in 2002 it returned a net loss of £119 million (Rexam, *Annual Report, 2003*).

Rexam's ability to work closely with its customers and respond to their packaging requirements has been critical to its survival and growth. Its top ten customers account for roughly one-half of its total revenues in consumer packaging (Rexam, *Annual Report, 2000*: 39). Rexam has close long-term relationships with its key customers such as Coca-Cola, PepsiCo, InBev, Anheuser-Busch, Carlsberg, Unilever and Heineken. In 2004, it produced around 52 billion beverage cans ('enough to stretch around the world 180 times if placed end-to-end'), of which it supplied the Coca-Cola system worldwide with around 20 billion (*FT*, 27 July 2005). It has introduced the most advanced technologies in the packaging industry in order to meet their needs: 'Creating great packaging can't be achieved by keeping us at arm's length, but rather by combining technical rigour with design flair' (Rexam website).

Primary metal supply

The metal can industry is a major consumer of both aluminium and steel. The manufacturers of the two metals are locked in intense competition for the massive global beverage can makers.

High-quality metal cans require high-quality supplies of both materials. To a considerable degree, can makers have been able to meet the stringent demands of the world's leading beverage companies for less expensive, lighter, more attractive, recyclable metal cans, through the technical progress achieved in the world's leading metals producers. This has necessitated the investment of large amounts in research and development. They have also needed to pursue greater size in order to benefit from economies of scale in procurement.

Alongside the growing concentration in the beverage industry, the other major users of primary metals have also consolidated at high speed during the global business revolution, including especially, the automobile industry, but also the aerospace industry (for aluminium), the construction industry and the household durable goods industries (for steel). Like the beverage industry, they demand continuous progress in the quality of their products and they place intense pressure for improvements in metal weight alongside improved technical performance and lower price. Both the steel industry and the aluminium industry have witnessed a period of unprecedented industrial concentration, as the industry leaders strive to win the competition for sales to global customers in the main consuming industries.

Aluminium

In the aluminium sheet industry, Alcoa and Alcan have emerged as the world's leading producers. The degree of market concentration at a global level increased greatly in recent years with Alcan's acquisition of Algroup (Switzerland) and Pechiney (France), and Alcoa's acquisition of Cordant and Reynolds. Between them they produce over two-fifths of global aluminium output (by weight): Alcoa produces around 29 per cent and Alcan around 13 per cent (company websites).

Steel

In the steel industry, recent years have seen a stream of giant mergers. The steel industry is generally regarded as highly fragmented: the top ten steel firms account for 'only' 27 per cent of global output in terms of weight (Nolan and Rui, 2004b). However, the industry leaders have focused on high value-added, high-technology products for global industry leaders in the automobile, metal can, household consumer goods and construction industries. Through their mergers and acquisitions (and divestments of poorly performing units) they have built powerful, industry-leading positions in their respective markets. For example, in the stainless steel industry, the top five firms account for 48 per cent of total value of global sales in the sector (Nolan and Rui, 2004b). The leading firms are all focused on high-technology products that have a high sales value and high profits per unit of physical weight. In terms of sales revenue, the world's top ten steel firms now account for almost two-thirds of total global sales revenue from the industry (see Table 4.8).

Mining

Consolidation in the steel industry has inter-acted symbiotically not only with growing consolidation in the main customer industries, but also with consolidation in its own supply chain, namely, the mining industry. The three emerging giants of the coal mining industry, Rio Tinto, BHP

Table 4.8 Sales revenue share by world ten largest steel producers (ranked by output) (US$ million)

Rank	1995			2003		
	Firms	Sales revenue	Employees	Firms	Sales revenue	Employees
1	Nippon Steel	30,614	36,316	Arcelor	31,836	98,264
2	POSCO	11,181	–	LNM	12,000	120,000
3	British Steel	11,032	39,800	Nippon	25,903	46,233
4	Usinor	15,719	58,335	JFE	22,672	54,100
5	Riva Group	4,474	–	POSCO	14,930	27,475
6	US Steel	6,872	20,831	Baosteel	14,548	102,039
7	NKK	18,711	39,603	Corus	14,640	49,400
8	Arbed	8,979	46,012	US Steel	9,458	47,000
9	Kawasaki Steel	12,064	30,711	Thyssen Krupp	39,188	190,102
10	Sumitomo Metal	14,830	15,448	Nucor	6,266	9,900
A	Revenue of the ten	134,476			191,441	
B	Revenue of world steel	250,000			300,000	
C	A/B	53%			64%	

Source: Nolan and Rui (2004b).
Notes: The data for Riva Group are for 1997, and for US Steel are for 1996. Employee data for NKK and Kawasaki Steel are for 2000, and for Sumitomo Metal are for 1997.

Billiton and Anglo American, emerged from massive asset reorganization in the industry through merger and acquisition and divestiture of non-core business. In 2001, together they accounted for 62 per cent of the total volume of globally traded coal (Nolan and Rui, 2004a). In the closely related iron ore industry, the three giants, namely CVRD, Rio Tinto and BHP Billiton, account for over one-half of all internationally traded iron ore (*FT*, 23 August 2004).

Glass bottles

Until the development of the metal beverage can in the 1950s, glass bottles were the only form of primary packaging in the beverage industry.[28] Like the beverage industry, the glass bottle industry was then highly fragmented, with thousands of small-scale local producers in every large country. However, in recent decades, the glass bottle industry has altered sharply. It has come under severe attack from alternative packaging materials, beginning with cans in the 1960s, then extending into plastic bottles, continuing with the development of reusable plastic bottles and continuing in the 1990s with the development of contour plastic bottles and metal contour/embossed cans. In high-income countries, soft drinks rarely use glass containers as the primary packaging. Glass came to be regarded as an unexciting package in the soft drinks industry around the world. Profits came under severe attack throughout the industry.

However, despite its relative decline, the glass bottle remained an important form of packaging. Even in high-income countries, it remains the main form of primary packaging for 'premium' beers, and in developing countries, it dominates primary packaging in the beer industry. In Asia and South America, around 65–70 per cent of beer is consumed in recyclable glass bottles, although in the United States, cans are the dominant form of packaging. In several developing countries, such as Mexico and the Philippines, it has remained an important form of packaging for soft drinks. Moreover, as we shall see, the glass bottle is making a comeback in soft drinks in developing countries such as China and India, in which it appeared to have been eclipsed by cans and PET.

Since the 1980s, the level of industrial concentration in the glass container industry has progressed rapidly. Transport costs have fallen, giving increased advantage to large plants. A large plant is now able to compete at distances up to 250 kilometres, and even 400–500 kilometres is now feasible. The emerging large glassmakers in the high-income countries each now has several large plants even within a single geographical territory such as Europe, typically in transition from many small plants to a smaller number of large plants, benefiting from economies of scale. Moreover, new technologies have increased the plant level economies of scale in the manufacture of glass bottles. In addition, privatization in both high-income countries (e.g., Saint-Gobain) and low-income countries, and elimination of restrictions on cross-border mergers and acquisitions, have contributed to dramatic institutional change in this, as in most industries, since the 1980s.

Following successive rounds of merger and acquisition in the 1990s, the glass bottle container industry in most advanced economies has become highly consolidated. Globally, the top ten firms are estimated to account for around three-quarters of total revenues in the sector. However, two firms stand out above the rest. Owens-Illinois is the world's largest glass bottle manufacturer. It is strongly focused on glass bottles, with an annual revenue of around US$ 6.2 billion in 2003

Table 4.9   Market share of the world's leading glass bottle manufacturers, 2003

	North America (%)	Europe (%)
Owens-Illinois	42	37
Saint-Gobain	31	24
Rexam	–	10
Anchor	20	–
Ardagh	–	24
Other	7	–

Sources: Owens-Illinois Presentation 'Public Presentation to Senior Lenders', February 2004 (*website*); Rexam 'US Investor Roadshow Presentation', March 2003.

(*Fortune*, 5 April 2004), and an estimated market share in glass bottle manufacture of 42 per cent in North America and 37 per cent in Europe (see Table 4.9). It claims to produce one half of all glass containers manufactured globally. It is closely followed by Saint-Gobain, which has an estimated market share of 37 per cent in North America and 24 per cent in Europe. In other words, these two super-giants of the industry together account for around two-thirds of global glass bottle production. Between them they produce more than 60 billion glass bottles annually (company websites),[29] that is to say, an average of around ten bottles for each person in the world.

Owens-Illinois

Owens-Illinois owns more than 140 manufacturing plants spanning five continents, and employs 30,000 people. It has built a set of long-term relationships with global customers, including Coca-Cola, PepsiCo, Anheuser-Busch, Heineken, SAB-Miller Brewery, Labatts, Johnson & Johnson, P&G, Unilever, Diageo, and Bacardi (Owens-Illinois, *Annual Report, 2003*). By having widely dispersed plants across the world, Owens-Illinois is able to provide a global service for its customers.

The company's origin dates back to 1903, when Michael Joseph Owens, a glass blower working for the New England Glass Company, invented the first automatic bottle-making machine and set up Owens Bottle Company. Owens' invention revolutionized the glass industry and laid the groundwork for future technological innovations. In 1929, Owens merged with Illinois Glass Company to form Owens-Illinois Glass Company, changing its name to Owens-Illinois Inc. in 1965.

Owens-Illinois has grown by aggressive acquisitions. Since 1991, the company has acquired 18 glass container businesses in 18 countries, the most important of which were ACI in 1991, BTR's packaging business in 1998 and BSN in 2003. The acquisition of ACI, Australia's largest glass bottle maker, gave Owens-Illinois increased access to many developing markets, including China, as well as enhanced presence in Australia. The 1998 acquisition of BTR's glass bottle business enabled Owens-Illinois to expand its operations into Australia, New Zealand, China, Indonesia, and elsewhere. In 2004, it invested US\$ 1.5 billion to acquire BSN Glasspack (France), the second largest glass container manufacturer in Europe. BSN owned 19 glass bottle factories across Europe, and had an annual revenue of around US\$ 1.6 billion. After these acquisitions, Owens-Illinois became the largest glass bottle manufacturer in the world, with pro-forma revenue of around US\$ 8 billion. Around 47 per cent of its sales are from North America, 37 per cent from Europe, with 10 and 6 per cent respectively from the Asia-Pacific region and South America. Over 70 per cent of Owens-Illinois' revenues are from glass containers.

For decades, Owens-Illinois has been at the forefront of technological change in the glass bottle industry, with an annual R&D expenditure of more than US\$ 40 million. It licences glass container proprietary technology to 21 companies in 23 countries and has plastic technical assistance agreements with 30 companies in 15 countries. It invests over US\$ 30 million per year in new plant and equipment, which has enabled its process technology to stay at the forefront of the industry.

Saint-Gobain

Saint-Gobain was founded in the late seventeenth century by the Colbert government as an early example of a national champion firm in Europe. By the 1980s, it was a powerful state-owned company. It was privatized in 1986. However, like many other leading French SOEs, the national government was determined to support the construction of a genuine globally competitive 'national champion' headquartered in France, with mainly French shareholders, and with ultimate control in the hands of French institutions.[30] Since privatization, Saint-Gobain has grown rapidly. This has been in part through organic growth, but mainly through an explosive process of mergers and acquisitions. Some of its leading acquisitions were Ball, and Foster Forbes (glass); Point P, Lapeyre, Jewson, Graham and Rass Karcher (building materials); Norton, Furon-Chemfab, and Holz and Magic (high-performance materials). However, there were numerous smaller acquisitions made each year since the 1980s. Saint-Gobain's revenues grew from €11.4 billion in 1994 to €19.6 billion in 2003. It has expanded its net income closely in line with its revenue growth: net income grew from €413 million in

1994 (3.6 per cent of revenues) to €1.1 billion in 2003 (5.6 per cent of revenues). Saint-Gobain currently spends around €300 million per year on R&D, and is a technological leader in most areas in which it operates.

Saint-Gobain has three main divisions: 'housing materials' accounts for around 52 per cent of its total revenues, 'glass' accounts for around 38 per cent, and 'high performance materials' accounts for around 11 per cent. As a result of Saint-Gobain's internal management and technical strengths, and the acquisition of numerous companies in different sectors, during the past two decades it has built itself into a highly internationalized company, with production and sales across the globe. Of its 173,000 employees, only 30 per cent work in France. Fifteen per cent are in North America, 11 per cent in the United Kingdom and the same proportion in Germany. Eight per cent work in South America and 7 per cent in the Asia-Pacific region. France now accounts for only one-third of Saint-Gobain's total revenues. The rest of Europe accounts for 44 per cent, North America for 19 per cent, and the 'rest of the world' for around 8 per cent.

Through strong internal management and technical capabilities, and through the acquisition of a succession of other companies, Saint-Gobain has built a powerful portfolio of businesses with a considerable degree of overlap in terms of the character of the business undertaken. For example, the glass division has strong connections with both the building and the high-performance materials divisions. Saint-Gobain is now the world leader in terms of market share in insulation materials; in flasks for fragrances, pharmaceuticals and medical products; in plastic pumps and dispensers; in industrial ceramics for thermal and mechanical applications; in abrasives; in ductile cast-iron pipes; and in ductile cast-iron roadwork components; in external insulation grids for buildings; and in glass threads for reinforcements. It is the joint world leader in roofing products; and in bottles and jars for food packaging (including beverages and miscellaneous food products). It is the world number two in flat glass, including glass for the building industry, the automotive industry and speciality purposes, such as aerospace, fireproof glass, nuclear safety, home appliances, and industrial refrigeration. It is the world number one or two for high-performance plastics. Saint-Gobain has been able to gain from economies of scale and scope in raising finance, branding, procurement, human resource management, research and development, managing sustainable development, and sales and marketing.

The glass division accounts for around 40 per cent of the company's total revenues, with a total revenue of around €11.3 billion in 2003.

However, unlike Owens-Illinois, which focuses strongly on glass bottles, Saint-Gobain's glass division is also the world leader in flat glass; in glass-based materials for insulation; glass threads; flasks for fragrances, pharmaceuticals and medical products; and plastic pumps and dispensers. It is the long-term partner for Airbus in the supply of aircraft windows. In 2003, Saint-Gobain's glass bottle and glass jar business had a revenue of €3.9 billion, making it the second largest producer globally after Owens-Illinois. It produces around 30 billion bottles per year. As we have seen (Table 4.9), it holds a 24 per cent market share in Europe and a 37 per cent market share in North America. Saint-Gobain's rapid growth in North America in the glass bottle market was largely due to its acquisition of the glass divisions of Ball and Foster Forbes, leading US glass bottle makers. The two entities were combined to form Ball Foster Glass.

PET bottles

Polyethylene terephthalate (PET) (plastic) bottles were developed in the late 1960s, and quickly became the most important form of primary packaging in the soft drinks industry. The technical challenges in the beer industry are greater than in soft drinks, and PET has a less important place in this industry. However, the leading PET manufacturers are devoting a lot of research activity to improving the capabilities of PET to cope with the specific requirements of the beer industry, and it is predicted that its share in this industry will rise significantly. Technology has advanced greatly. Packaging became stronger and less liable to breakage. It enabled the product to have a longer storage life without product deterioration. PET bottles became steadily lighter, thus reducing energy costs per unit manufactured and transported. Walls became thinner. New shapes allowed the use of more efficient packing methods. Stronger forms of PET enabled multiple reuse of washable, refillable bottles.

The manufacture of PET bottles at the global level has not seen the degree of industrial concentration that has emerged in the can making or glass bottle industry, where a small number of firms dominate the production of these products for the world's leading firms. This is, in part, related to the specific technical characteristics of this industry. The supply chain is more extended and complex than that involved in either metal cans or glass bottles. Bottle-grade PET resin is produced from PTA, which is manufactured by petrochemical firms. This is supplied to an entity that manufactures PET 'pre-forms', so-called because they are small tubes, a few inches long, 'pre-formed' and ready for 'blowing' into the specified shape of the particular bottle. The 'blowing' process involves the transformation of the small 'pre-form' into a full-sized and shaped bottle. Resin is a key part of the supply chain, since it accounts for around 50–60 per cent of the total cost of producing PET bottles. The manufacture of both pre-forms and their conversion into PET bottles involves relatively large investments in complex, high-technology equipment. There are considerable economies of scale in both of these parts of the supply chain. However, in principle, either the pre-form manufacturing and or the converters may be owned and operated by an independent firm or by the bottlers themselves.

PET manufacturers typically undertake both the extrusion of PET 'pre-forms' and the 'blowing' of pre-forms into the final bottle. A significant minority of beverage plants produce their own PET bottles in-house (see Table 4.10).

In recent years, within that part of the supply of bottles that is purchased from independent 'converters' or 'blowing' companies, the industry has become more concentrated. This follows a series of divestments of non-core PET businesses by diversified firms and their amalgamation into relatively large participants in the PET industry through mergers and acquisitions. By 2003, excluding the production for self-consumption, the top four firms accounted for almost two-thirds of the total production of PET bottles in North America and Europe respectively (see Table 4.10).

Table 4.10 Market share of main PET bottle manufacturers, 2003 (% of resin consumption)

	North America	Europe
Amcor	21	18
Alpla	–	11
Constar	11	8
Owens-Illinois	10	–
Plastipak	9	–
Resinex	–	4
Ball	5	–
Graham	5	–
Others	21	22
Self-manufacture	18	37
Share of top four firms	51	41
Share of top four firms in externally purchased PET bottles	62	65

Source: Ball Corporation (2004); *Creating Global Leadership*, Amcor Investment Prospectus, May 2002: 5.

A large part of the technical progress in the PET bottle industry is achieved by the upstream chemical companies that manufacture bottle-grade PET resin,[31] as well as by the downstream manufacturers of pre-form and blowing equipment. However, there are still some significant economies of scale in the production of PET bottles. Larger firms buy more pre-form and blowing machines, which means that they tend to obtain their equipment at a lower unit cost. Lower unit resin costs obtained through central procurement of larger quantities of resin can substantially increase overall profitability. However, in their efforts to reduce system costs, large beverage manufacturers have increasingly negotiated directly with resin suppliers in order to obtain lower costs. This enables them to control more tightly the margin that PET makers can achieve.

There are intense pressures on the PET firms arising from the high degree of concentration in the global beverage industry, as well as from their high degree of dependence on the price of PET resin. There are relatively high transport costs associated with moving PET bottles over long distances. Therefore, the normal arrangement is for PET manufac-turers to produce both pre-forms and the blown bottles either very close to the customer or 'in-line' within the customer's own plant. Whole production lines are often tied to a particular customer, and often with contracts of several years' duration. For example, Plastipack has long-standing supply relationships with Kraft (15 years), PepsiCo (15 years) and Procter and Gamble (25 years). Larger PET firms are able to build a set of plants located in or close to their customers, which may enable them to offer a lower unit price to the customer. PET manufacturers tend to be highly dependent on a small number of customers, due especially to the high levels of concentration in the global beverage industry. For example, Constar's (see below) top five customers account for 56 per cent of its total sales, with Coca-Cola and PepsiCo accounting for 34 per cent and 11 per cent respectively (Constar, *Annual Report, 2004*). The top ten customers of Plastipak account for 69 per cent of its revenue (Plastipak, *Annual Report, 2003*), and Procter and Gamble alone accounts for 27 per cent of its revenues.

Amcor

Amcor has established itself as by far the global industry leader, accounting for around one-quarter of the total supply of purchased PET bottles in North America and Europe (Amcor, *Annual Report, 2004*). Up until the early 1990s, Amcor, based in Australia, had been a diversi-fied packaging and paper materials company. In the mid-1990s, it decided to build itself into a focused packaging company. It divested its holdings in non-core businesses, and began a series of acquisitions. Its major acquisitions were the PET business of Schmalbach-Lubeca, bought for US$ 2.9 billion in 2002, and Alcoa's Latin American PET business, bought for US$ 115 million in 2003. Amcor now has almost 40 plants in 20 countries worldwide making PET bottles and 15 making closures. Amcor's total revenues in 2003 were US$ 7 billion, of which its PET bottles and closures amounted to around US$ 2.5 billion, with profits (EBITDA) from this business segment of around US$ 200 million. Amcor is the technical leader in the PET industry, with annual R&D expenditure of around US$ 60 million. It has been in the lead in developing new multi-layer 'barrier' technologies.[32] In the four years 1999–2003, Schmalbach invested more than US$ 600 million in upgrading its manufacturing facilities. In 2003 alone, it spent around US$ 200 million on capital equipment, including the purchase of 26 injection moulding machines and 29 blowing machines. Amcor now accounts for over one-quarter of the total market for PET bottles (excluding self-produced PET) in North America and Europe.

Other firms
There are several second tier firms in the industry (see Table 4.10). They include Constar, Owens-Illinois, Alpla, Plastipak and Rexam. Constar is the closest competitor to Amcor. It formed a part of Crown Holdings from 1992 until 2003, when Crown sold 90 per cent of its interest in the company. It has PET revenues of around US$ 750 million, and accounts for around 13 per cent of the market in both North America and Europe (excluding self-production). Owens-Illinois is not only the world's leading manufacturer of glass bottles, it is also a major producer of PET in North America, with around 12 per cent of the market, excluding self-production by beverage makers. In 2003, it had sales of around US$ 1.9 billion from its PET division, with profits (EBITDA) of around US$ 658 million from PET. Alpla is wholly focused on PET. It is the second largest PET firm in Europe, with revenue of €1.3 billion in 2003. It has 80 blowing facilities around the world, including almost 30 in Germany, France, the United Kingdom and Italy. It is also growing fast in Latin America, with 20 blowing facilities in the region. Plastipak has around 11 per cent of the North American market, excluding self-production. In 2003, it had revenues of US$ 890 million, and profits (EBITDA) of US$ 102 million. Although it is still a relatively small part of its total business (see above), Rexam is nevertheless an important player in the manufacture of plastic bottles for CSDs, fruit drinks,

mineral water and beer. Like the other leading packaging firms, Rexam has a relatively high level of innovative capability.

Rexam has played a leading role in the development of PET beer bottles. Their use is still in its infancy. However, they have substantial advantages over other types of packaging, especially light-weighting. In the past few years, the global leading packaging manufacturers have competed with each other in the use of advanced technologies to develop PET beer bottles. For instance, Rexam has patented active barrier technology that removes any oxygen penetration in the multi-layer PET bottle. Rexam is the world's only manufacturer of refillable PEN (polyethylene naphthalate) beer bottles. Refillable PEN beer bottles possess many of the qualities of glass, but with the benefits of plastic. Refillable PEN bottles have substantial environmental advantages, in that single bottles can run up to 20 trips on existing return system lines. They have excellent barrier properties that minimize intrusion by oxygen, carbon dioxide and ultraviolet light. This characteristic is highly important because beer goes bad quickly when it is exposed to oxygen, carbon dioxide and ultraviolet light. PEN bottles, like glass bottles, can be pasteurized, and the washing temperatures can go as high as 85 degrees centigrade. A PEN bottle is much lighter than a glass bottle, and has the safety benefits of plastic. PEN is also more suitable for special consumption venues such as bars. The shelf life of a PEN bottle can be as long as six months. In terms of capping, PEN bottles are little different from glass bottles: the closure type can be either a crown, tear-off or screw cap. In the long run, refillable PEN is likely to be of central importance in the beer industry, especially as it has the advantage of being compatible with existing glass return systems and filling lines. Its current use in Norway and Denmark is thought likely to spread much more widely, in which case Rexam's technology will be a major competitive advantage.

4.3.2 PET machinery

The main body of technical progress in the PET bottle industry has been achieved by the specialist machine builders that make two different types of machinery, namely 'pre-forms' and the equipment that 'blows' the pre-forms into their final bottle form. Each of these highly specialized areas is dominated by a tiny number of firms. Barriers to entry in these areas are high. The machinery makers coordinate their technical progress closely with the world's leading beverage companies, which set the industry standards for PET bottles, and have an intense interest in all aspects of technical progress in the PET bottle industry.

Pre-form machines: Husky

Today, the global market for all types of pre-form PET injection moulding machines, including both high- and low-volume machines, is estimated to be around US$ 2 billion. By the late 1970s, Husky (Canada) was already the world's leading manufacturer of high technology, high-volume injection moulding machines. It has annual revenues of around US$ 800 million, almost entirely derived from PET injection-moulding machinery. It accounts for 76 per cent of the total global market for high volume PET injection machines (Husky, *Annual Report, 2003*). This is the segment of the sector that sells machines for the most demanding global customers, who are mainly in the beverage industry. The average cost of a single Husky pre-form machine is around US$ 1.6 million. Husky invests more than US$ 20 million per year in R&D. It holds over 185 patents covering the most important aspects of innovation in the PET industry. Its main customers have remorselessly pushed Husky to develop lighter weight forms of PET that are consistent with maintaining the physical integrity of the bottle.

The main focus of Husky's technical progress has been its injection moulding machines. One of the main areas of advance has been in building machines with an increasing number of 'cavities' (individual moulds). In 1979, Husky introduced 12- and 16-cavity moulds. In the following years, it introduced injection machines with an ever-increasing number of cavities. By 2003, it had introduced an injection machine with 144 cavities. Larger machines are able to produce a correspondingly greater output per hour. Today, Husky's smallest machine for producing 591-ml (the popular US 20-oz size) CSD pre-forms has 32 cavities, producing around 10,000 units of pre-forms per hour. The 144-cavity machine for the same bottle type produces almost 50,000 per hour.

Husky has many other technical advances in products that are closely associated with its main business of making injection machines for PET bottles. As well as being the world's leading supplier of injection machines for pre-forms for PET bottles, Husky also has a leading position in the supply of injection equipment to make plastic closures, especially for beverage bottles, but also for other products. Husky has developed the 'hot runner' system which delivers plastic from the machine nozzle to the mould cavity, which can be incorporated into the PET injection moulding machines to improve their technical efficiency. Hot runners help to improve product quality while reducing material use and energy consumption per pre-form. One of the most dynamic parts of Husky's market for hot runners is East Asia, especially China. This has contributed to Husky's decision to build a technical centre in Shanghai, which was completed in 2004. This is already manufacturing hot runners, as well as having other manufacturing and service functions. Husky is the world's number one producer of hot runners, and supplies 100 per cent of the hot runners used in China.

Blowing equipment: Sidel

By the late 1980s, the French company Sidel had become the world leader in PET blowing equipment. By the end of the 1990s, it had accounted for an estimated 55 per cent of the total global market (Sidel, *Annual Report, 1998*). Among its notable achievements was the penetration of the North American market, where it is the market leader. The carbonated soft drinks segment is its main target market, accounting for about two-thirds of its total sales. Almost all of the blowing equipment acquired by the Coca-Cola system and its suppliers in China in the 1990s was purchased from Sidel. It is also the world's leading designer and manufacturer of moulds for PET bottles. It runs the world's largest mould production plant. Sidel has its own complex value chain. It outsources the manufacture of components and sub-assembly to over 250 selected subcontractors. Sidel undertakes the research and development for technical progress in its machines; designs and markets them, tests them, and conducts the final customizing and production of moulds. Sidel's technical progress helped to produce a 30–45 per cent reduction in the weight of PET bottles from the late 1980s to the late 1990s.

By the late 1990s, Sidel had become a truly global company with 18 manufacturing units and 32 service centres in 25 countries. Its products are sold in 131 countries. Apart from its plants in France, it has production facilities in the United States, Canada, Chile, Brazil, Germany, Spain, Malaysia and China. During 2003 alone, seven new subsidiaries were set up in Vienna, Newbury (UK), Moscow, Dubai, Bangkok, Chengdu (China) and Sydney. It employs 3,800 people and has 12 R&D centres worldwide.

A large blowing facility embodies sophisticated engineering technology, and costs around US$ 6–7 million. Sidel has been at the forefront of technical progress in this field since the initial launch of plastic bottles in the beverage industry: 'Virtually every major invention in stretch blow-moulding has come from Sidel, which has set many new standards in plastic packaging solutions'. It spends about 3 per cent of its annual sales revenue on R&D, employing 250 people in its research centres located in France, Canada, India and the United States. In the late 1990s, it spent annually around €28 million on research and development. Its equipment has consistently incorporated new technical capabilities that facilitate 'light-weighting' of PET bottles and permit larger numbers of pre-forms to be blown per hour. Its latest blowers (the SBO Series Two-Plus) are estimated to reduce blowing costs per unit by around 10 per cent.

In 2003, Tetra Laval, the packaging giant, acquired Sidel. With the weight of Tetra Laval behind it, Sidel will be in an even better position to maintain its leading position in the global PET pre-form blowing industry.

Tetra Laval

Tetra Laval is a private company owned by the Swedish-based Raussing family. The company is headquartered in Switzerland. Tetra Pak began in the early 1950s as one of the first packaging companies to develop an alternative to the glass bottle for the distribution of liquid milk. Since then, it has become one of the world's largest suppliers of packaging systems for milk, fruit juices and drinks, and many other products. In 1991, Tetra Pak merged with Alfa Laval, a world leader in plant engineering and the manufacture of equipment for liquid food processing, especially dairy products, and cheese making.

Tetra Laval has long had a firm focus on its core business, packaging. The group's acquisition of Sidel has made it an even more powerful firm in this industry (see above). It now is able to provide a wide range of different types of packaging equipment, from cartons to PET bottles and closures. Tetra Laval employs more than 29,000 people in over 165 countries and has 41 research centres globally (Tetra Laval, *Annual Report, 2004*). It is organized around three autonomous industry groups: Tetra Pak, DeLaval and Sidel. In 2003, Tetra Laval generated a revenue of €8.7 billion, with Tetra Pak accounting for €7.3 billion, with DeLaval and Sidel each accounting for €710 million. Tetra Pak is truly global. It has 15 assembly plants, 59 service centres and 47 sales offices located around the world, serving more than 165 countries. A key strategy has been to achieve and sustain long-term partnerships with leading global firms in the dairy and beverage industries.

Tetra Laval believes that long-term success depends on its capability to develop new products. Only in this way does it feel that it can sustain its leading position in processing and packaging innovation. Each of Tetra Laval's divisions pays special attention to R&D. The company spends about 3 per cent of its annual sales on research.

4.3.3   Filling equipment

The global market for filling equipment is dominated by two German firms, Krones and KHS's, whose combined share is around 44 per cent (28 per cent and 16 per cent respectively) (Krones and KHS, *Annual*

Reports, 2003). However, within the high-technology, high value-added segment for leading global customers, their share is considerably higher. The world's leading beverage companies have bought machines almost exclusively from these two companies because of their high levels of reliability, low operating costs, high speed, more consistent filling height, and low rates of damage to bottles and product. The high-technology filling machines produced by KHS and Krones can sell for up to US$ 5 million each. Krones and KHS estimate that they account for 50 per cent and 35 per cent respectively of global sales of high-speed beverage bottling lines.

In the European market for bottling line equipment, Krones accounts for around 50 per cent, compared with around 30–35 per cent for KHS and around 20 per cent for Sasib, the Italian machine-building company, which has been taken over by SIG (Swiss International Group). The US market also is dominated by Krones and KHS. Only the Japanese market eludes them, which is mainly supplied by Mitsubishi and Dai Nippon.

In the brewing industry, the high value-added, high-technology segments of the market are dominated by the global leaders. In the supply of bottling lines for 'premium' beers, the two global leaders, KHS and Krones, account for around 90 per cent of the total market. Many of their technical developments have become industry standards.

KHS

KHS is one of the global leading firms in the manufacture of packaging equipment. It designs, manufactures, and installs packaging lines for consumer goods industries from beer, soft drinks, water, juice, wine and liquor, to milk, vinegar, and oil. It can supply entire packaging lines, from cleaning, filling, inspecting, labelling and pasteurizing to packaging, palletizing, filtering and conveying. It employs 3,000 people globally, of which 2,000 are in Germany and 1,000 in Brazil and the United States. Its customers include many global giants, such as Coca-Cola, Anheuser-Busch, InBev, Danone and Campbell.

KHS was formed in 1993 as a result of a merger of three leading German packaging equipment manufacturers, AG Holstein, SEN and Klöckner-Werke.[33] It subsequently acquired Kisters Maschinenbau, Alfill Engineering and Metec. The beer sector accounts for over 60 per cent of KHS's total revenues. Carbonated soft drinks are the company's second largest business segment, followed by water, wine and fruit juice. Between 1998 and 2003, KHS's sales revenue rose from €464 million to €675 million. In 2003, it generated operating profits before tax of €17 million.

Thereafter, KHS expanded through both organic growth and acquisitions. In 1999, it acquired Kisters. Kisters is well known in the global beverage industry for producing ultra-modern packaging systems. In 2003, it acquired Alfill Engineering and Metec. Alfill possesses a strong competitive advantages in dry PET bottle and cap sterilization. Metec is Europe's leading supplier of crate-sorting equipment and also plays a leading role, among other things, in the field of PET bottle sorting. The acquisition of Metec has further strengthened KHS's position in the area of quality assurance systems. These acquisitions have helped to make KHS one of the global leading firms in manufacturing complete packaging lines for consumer goods industries. It has also recently acquired Bartelt, a packaging machines manufacturer for the candy, food, and semi-luxury industries in Florida.

Between 1998 and 2003, KHS achieved rapid growth alongside stagnation in the German economy. In this period, sales revenue rose from €464 million to €675 million, while the number of employees rose from 2,500 to 3,133 in the same period. In 2003, KHS generated operating profits before tax of €17 million.

KHS is highly focused on the field of equipment for bottle filling, washing and labelling. It prides itself on its high technical level with a consistent innovation record. As well as having a strong in-house research capability, it cooperates closely with leading German universities on research and development. Many of its innovations have become industrial standards. For example, its new Innofill DRV-VF system is the 'first computer-controlled, volumetric filling system capable of filling carbonated and non-carbonated beverages in plastic bottles using only two pneumatically actuated membrane cylinders to lift as well as press bottles and seal bottle mouths against the filling valve' (KHS website news).

Krones

KHS's main international competitor is another German firm, Krones, which also specializes in manufacturing the entire packaging lines. It also serves a similar range of beverage industries, and competes for the same global clients. However, KHS' history extends back to the late nineteenth century, while Krones only entered the packaging field in the early 1950s. KHS is a private company, while Krones is listed on the Frankfurt Stock Exchange. Krones is more than twice as large as KHS in terms of revenue, with an annual revenue of around €2 billion. Over the past five years, Krones' revenue has grown even faster than that of KHS.

Krones is also highly focused on the filling line industry, which accounts for over 80 per cent of its total sales revenue of €1.44 billion (Krones, *Annual Report, 2003*). Since the early 1990s, Krones has acquired Kettner, Kosme, Sander Hansen and Steineker Syskron. It spends around 6–7 per cent of its revenues on research and development. Thirty-five per cent of its sales are from Europe, 28 per cent from North America and 37 per cent from the Asia-Pacific region (including Japan and China). It employs almost 9,000 people, including around 1,000 system engineers, who work with its customers to devise the blueprints for the finished machine. Krones has consistently held at least a quarter of the global market for filling machines since the early 1990s, growing and advancing technologically alongside the global expansion of demand for beverages.

4.3.4 Ingredients: carbon dioxide

Until recently, the industrial gases sector was highly fragmented globally, with most firms in the industry confined to national markets. Generally, gases need to be produced close to the customer. In high-income countries, it is not feasible to transport gases more than around 200 kilometres and still provide a competitive price to the customer. In developing countries with less highly developed transport systems, the distances over which industrial gas producers can compete is much smaller. However, there are strong economies of scale in this industry. Changes in technology have led to increased plant level economies of scale. Large companies enjoy competitive advantages due to procurement economies from their supply chain. For example, in the United Kingdom alone, BOC has around 2,000 trucks, and perhaps as many as 10,000 trucks globally, which provides a large opportunity to lower unit costs in truck purchase compared to smaller firms in the sector. Well-targeted acquisitions can increase firm's technical capabilities. Large firms can enjoy advantages in terms of their ability to fund technical progress and through establishing global partnerships with their main customers. The major customers for industrial gases include the steel industry, oil and petrochemicals, food and beverages, and medical services. Safety is a critically important issue in the transport and use of industrial gases. The global giants have established control systems and reputations as safe operators, which is a significant advantage over smaller competitors. Large global users of industrial gases are acutely safety-conscious, and the safety reputation of the supplier of industrial gases is a key factor in competitive advantage.

Since the 1980s, this sector has undergone high-speed international consolidation. The leading national firms have turned into global leaders through extensive mergers and acquisitions. The four leading firms may now account for as much as 80 per cent of total global sales of industrial gases.

Air Liquide

The global leader, Air Liquide, based in France, has grown into the world's leading supplier of industrial gases. By 2003, it had revenues of around US$ 10 billion, with 64 per cent of its revenues from Europe, 21 per cent from the Americas, and 13 per cent from the Asia-Pacific region. It spends around US$ 180 million on R&D. Among its technical advances are systems that allow for full traceability of carbon dioxide supplies to carbonated beverage manufacturers such as Coca-Cola. It has a global market share of around 25 per cent in industrial gases (see Table 4.11). In 2004, it expanded its reach in industrial gases still further by completing the acquisition of its German rival Messer Greisheim for US$ 3.3 billion (*FT*, 7 September 2004).

BOC

Of the leading industrial gas firms, BOC is the most truly global. Twenty-seven per cent of its total revenues come from Europe, 20 per cent from the Americas and 31 per cent from the Asia-Pacific region (BOC, *Annual Report, 2003*). Its most important acquisition was made relatively early. In 1978 it purchased Airco (USA), which doubled its size. It has a close relationship with NuCO2, in which it has a 13 per cent equity share. NuCO2 is the largest supplier of CO2 and carbonating

Table 4.11   Global market share in industrial gases, 2003

	Sales of industrial gases (US$ billion)	Market share (%)
Total global market	36.0[a]	100
Air Liquide	8.9	25
BOC	7.7	22
Linde	6.0	17
Praxair	5.6	16

Source: Derived from annual reports of Air Liquide, Linde, Praxair and BOC
Note: [a] industrial gases only. Linde's total revenue in 2003 was around US$ 11 billion, which included US$ 3.6 in sales of forklift trucks

systems to the fountain beverage industry in the United States. BOC has acquired a succession of industrial gas businesses in developing countries. By 2003, it employed round 43,000 people, of which over 7,000 are in the Asia-Pacific region, and generated revenues of US$ 7.7 billion. It spends around US$ 40–50 million annually on R&D.

Linde

Linde, based in Germany, grew through a succession of international mergers and acquisitions, including the purchase of the Dutch and Swedish market leaders, Hoek and Aga respectively. By 2003, Linde was a giant of the global industrial gases sector, with revenues of US$ 6 billion (excluding its large business in forklift trucks) and 47,000 employees worldwide. Linde is closely followed by US-based Praxair, with revenues of close to US$ 6 billion.

4.3.5 Advertising and marketing

The total global 'media' spend in 2003 was estimated to be over US$ 1 trillion, including both 'specialist communications' (US$ 732 billion) and advertising (US$ 326 billion) (Sorrell, 2005). The sector has witnessed intense merger and acquisition activity. By 2001, the top four advertising and communications companies (WPP, Omnicom, Interpublic, and Publicis) accounted for 56 per cent of total global advertising revenue (Merrill Lynch, 2002). The advertising and communications industry has become polarized into a small number of immensely powerful firms and a large number of small firms.[34] The industry has negligible 'research and development' expenditure. It has a relatively small level of investment in fixed assets. Few ordinary people have heard of the leading firms.

However, the forces driving forward industry consolidation have much in common with those affecting other sectors. Their potential markets have swelled enormously since the 1980s. The leading firms do have 'brand' among their customers, in the sense that the industry leaders are recognized as able to provide a reliable service in assembling a large package of interrelated 'products' that can be 'distributed to meet their customers needs across the world'. Once the leaders have established their 'brand' among their leading customers, it constitutes an important barrier to entry to other media firms. The customer base of advertising and communications firms is consolidating remorselessly, and 'it is no surprise that agencies are also consolidating' (Sorrell, 2005). The world's top ten spenders on advertising average US$ 2.5 billion per company (Sorrell, 2005). The top ten clients account for 19 per cent of the revenue of Omnicom (Omnicom, *Annual Report, 2004*). The top 20 clients account for 30 per cent of Interpublic's revenue (Interpublic, *Annual Report, 2004*). Interpublic's top five clients[35] account for 17.4 per cent of its revenue. For WPP, the top 40 clients account for 40 per cent of its revenue (WPP, *Annual Report, 2004*). They seek advertising and communications firms that combine global scale with an ability to integrate global 'messages' into a specific local context. The leading advertising and communications firms combine economies of scale with the specialist capabilities of numerous semi-autonomous subsidiaries, each with their own distinctive areas of competence and their own distinctive industry 'brand'. While the headquarters works with the head office on global aspects of advertising and communications services, the local subsidiaries can organize the 'local' aspects.

Advertising and communications companies have their own procurement supply chain. They need to negotiate with innumerable small and medium-sized firms, as well as some large firms, that supply them with a wide range of 'inputs', including IT hardware and software, and financial services. On the 'creative' side, such as film production companies that make advertisements and other media communications products, 'voracious procurement departments . . . are driving consolidation' (Sorrell, 2005). In the media industry, the global business revolution has witnessed the emergence of giant media empires, including News International, Time Warner, Viacom, and Disney. In 2002, the four leading advertising and marketing companies (Omnicom, Publicis, WPP and Interpublic) spent between US\$ 22 and 35 billion on media buying, accounting for around 43 per cent of the total spending of the whole industry (*FT*, 13 June 2002). Such massive spending power greatly increased their leverage with the giant global media companies.[36]

4.3.6   Trucks

The world's leading beverage companies are among the largest purchasers of trucks, either directly, or through their 'third-party' logistics suppliers. Most beverages are delivered to customers by truck. The fleets operated by global industry leaders are enormous. For example, in the late 1990s, Coca-Cola bottlers across the world operated more than 200,000 vehicles, forming one of the world's largest trucking fleets (Nolan, 1998). Specialist third-party trucking companies working for Coca-Cola operated a further 230,000 trucks globally. Increasingly, leading beverage companies have centralized the procurement of trucks at a national, regional or even global level, in order to obtain better terms from the truck manufacturers, and to enable the trucks to have features that suit the particular customer.

The world's leading truck manufacturers obtain large benefits from supplying large orders from leading beverage companies. However, they also experience intense pressure from them to lower costs and improve technologies. This intensifies the pressure to increase scale in order to achieve greater volume of procurement and push down costs across their own value chains, including suppliers of truck components (engines, brake systems, tyres, exhaust systems, seats, informatics, and ventilation systems) and materials (steel, aluminium and plastics). Greater scale also enables them to achieve faster technical progress through economies of scope (coordinated technical progress that can be used in different divisions of the company), in order to provide the customer with more reliability, lower fuel costs, greater safety and more effective ability to meet pollution control requirements.

From the early 1990s on, industrial concentration in the truck industry greatly increased. The number of truck makers fell from more than 40 in 1975 to less than 20 in the late 1990s. By the late 1990s, the world's top five truck makers accounted for 54 per cent of total global sales in terms of the number of units sold (Nolan, 2001a: 518). However, in terms of total value, the share was considerably higher than this, as the leading truck companies tended to produce far higher technology vehicles. A heavy-duty truck produced by one of the top manufacturers can cost more then US$ 100,000, compared with a few thousand dollars for a small car or a low-technology truck produced by a developing country truck maker.

DaimlerChrysler emerged from the hectic period of consolidation in the industry as by far the most powerful firm in the industry. In the mid-1990s, Daimler acquired Freightliner, a leading US truck company. The merger of Daimler-Benz and Chrysler in 1998 accelerated dramatically consolidation in the truck industry. DaimlerChrysler became by far the largest truck and bus maker in the world. Following the merger, it produced almost 300,000 trucks annually, amounting to around 20 per cent of total world production in terms of number of units sold, and considerably more in terms of value of sales (Nolan, 2001a). By 2003, DaimlerChrysler's truck division had revenues of US$ 35.9 billion and operating profits of US$ 1.08 billion. The truck division alone spent US$ 1.3 billion on R&D. It employed 95,000 people globally. In 2003 it produced over 500,000 vehicles, with a market share of 21 per cent in Europe and 26 per cent in North America (Euromonitor).

Following industry consolidation in the 1990s, just three companies controlled the North American truck market. The other two North American giants of the industry, Navistar and Paccar also each occupied around one quarter of the North American truck market, so that between them the three giant truck companies accounted for over three-quarters of the market. Paccar was also a major player in Europe through its acquisition of Foden and Leyland (UK), and DAF (Netherlands), each of which was a 'national champion'. By 2003, Paccar occupied also 21 per cent of the UK market, as well as having strong positions in other European markets (Euromonitor).

In 1999, Volvo took the dramatic decision to sell its world-famous Volvo saloon vehicles division to Ford, and focus on the heavy-duty truck industry. Following the abortive attempt to merge with Scania, Volvo acquired Renault's heavy truck division, which had itself merged with Mack trucks in the United States. Volvo Trucks is now the world's third largest producer of heavy-duty trucks, with an output of 104,515 units in 2005 (Volvo, *Annual Report, 2005*). Volvo has a market share of 10 per cent in North America, 16 per cent in Western Europe and 25 per cent in Brazil (Volvo website).

In the early 1990s, General Motors was only a medium-sized player in the truck industry. However, it held a significant ownership share in Isuzu, the largest Japanese truck maker. In 1999, GM took advantage of the weakness of Isuzu in the wake of the Asian crisis, by raising its ownership share in Isuzu from 19 per cent to 50 per cent, so that Isuzu essentially became a part of GM. General Motors-Isuzu was now one of the world giants of the truck industry.

4.3.7   Retail

Pressure for consolidation within the beverage industry has not only arisen from economies of scale in 'upstream' procurement, but also from institutional transformation among the customers on the 'down-stream' side. The period since the 1980s has seen high-speed growth of beverage companies' customers, not only in the retail sector, but also in food services and entertainment, as well as sectors such as oil and petro-chemicals, where the leading companies sell a large volume of food and beverages in their retail outlets.

Food retailing has changed beyond recognition since the 1980s (see chapter 5). In most European countries, a handful of giant retail stores now occupies a large fraction of the market for beverage sales. More-over, the leading firms have entered a period of unprecedented mergers and acquisitions, often across national boundaries. There are now more than 30 giant retailers with annual revenues of over US$ 10 billion, including six 'super-giants' with revenues of over US$ 50 billion (*Fortune*, 26 July 2004). The world's largest firm is a retailer, Wal-Mart, with revenues of US$ 263 billion in 2003, and profits of over US$ 9 billion (*Fortune*, 26 July 2004). Wal-Mart's procurement power is enormous. For example, PepsiCo sells almost US$ 3 billion-worth of products to Wal-Mart annually, amounting for around 10 per cent of its total global revenues (PepsiCo, *Annual Report, 2004*).

4.4 Summary

This chapter has examined the profound changes affecting the global beverage value chain during the epoch of the global business revolution. In contrast to the simple, unchanging nature of beverages, the structure of the global beverage value chain is highly complex and dynamic. The beverage value chain spans a large number of global industries, including concentrate manufacturing, consumer packaging, metal manufacturing, mining, machinery manufacturing, advertising, trucks, logistics, and retail. Standing in the centre of this gigantic web of business relationships are a few large, globally branded beverage and food companies, each possessing enormous spending power. Together, they command dominating shares of the global market for their respective beverage segments. They have proactively selected and cultivated strategic value chain partners that can work with them to reduce cost and expand globally, while placing stringent demands on quality and cost. Spurred on by intensified competition at the global level, they have played a critical role in initiating and coordinating technological progress in the beverage value chain. The linkages between the systems integrator and its core strategic partners have clearly transcended the simple price relationship. The case of the Coca-Cola Company clearly illustrates the role of a systems integrator and the nature of strategic business relationships in the global beverages value chain.

Intensified demands and planning efforts from the systems integrators have resulted in the 'cascade effect' in the global beverage value chain. Pressures for consolidation, which allows for cost reduction and enhances capabilities for innovation, have built up at almost every level of the value chain, one after another. Leading firms in the beverage value chain engaged in massive restructuring and M&A activities, shedding off non-strategic assets while building up core competencies. This has resulted in a few capable firms from high-income countries dominating every high value-added segment of the beverage supply chain. In contrast to the everyday brands of the systems integrators, these are firms that most people have never heard of. However, they are usually also global companies that generate billions of dollars in annual revenues. They are able to invest significant resources in technological progress and expand with the systems integrators across the world. They have developed through long years of collaboration with the systems integrators and have formed valuable partnerships with the former that are extremely hard to replace.

5
The Retail Industry

Retail is an extraordinarily large and important industry. It is usually the largest industry in the economy in terms of turnover and employment. In the United States, the retail industry generated sales of US$ 3.7 trillion in 2003, or 34 per cent of the country's GDP, while representing about 12 per cent of the non-farm workforce in the United States.[37] This exceeded the number of workers in the US manufacturing sector as a whole. In addition, the importance of retail stems from its basic function as a market maker for manufacturers and their end consumers in the economy. The International Mass Retail Association (IMRA) described the strategic importance of the retail industry in its testimony to the US Congress:

> 'without retailers, wholesalers and consumers, manufacturers would have no markets... The distribution industry... makes the consumer market... Manufacturers are inherently linked to the industries that create and serve the markets – industries like retailing, wholesaling, warehousing, distribution, transportation, advertising and marketing. Indeed, manufacturers (especially those making consumer products) *depend* on the retail sector' (IMRA, 2003).

During the global business revolution, the global retail industry has undergone profound changes at every level of its value chain.

5.1 Consolidation among systems integrators

At the end of the twentieth century, global consumer spending is concentrated in a handful of high-income countries. In 1998, the top 20 retail markets in the world commanded total consumer spending of

Table 5.1   Global concentration of consumer spending, 1998

	Consumer spending (US$ billion)	% of total top 20 countries
United States	5,809	37
Japan	2,802	18
Germany	1,237	8
France	872	6
United Kingdom	860	6
Italy	723	5
Total: top six countries	12,303	80
Top 20 countries	15,558	100

Source: Goldman Sachs Investment Research, October 1999.

US$ 15.6 trillion.[38] Just six countries, that is, the United States, Japan, Germany, France, the United Kingdom and Italy, accounted for US$ 12.3 trillion or 80 per cent of the total consumer spending of the top 20 retail markets (see Table 5.1). For much of the twentieth century, retailing had been predominantly a domestic activity. Strong local regulations and differentiation in consumer preferences had limited the scale and scope of retail operations. Despite these constraints, the past two decades saw dramatic changes in the structure of retail industries in high-income countries, leading to the rise of giant, multinational retail operations.

Modern retail operations are susceptible to large economies of scale and scope in branding, technology investments, procurement, overseas sourcing and product development. In 2002, the top eight department stores in the United States together spent US$ 5.2 billion on advertising.[39] In order to leverage economies of scale in branding, the largest department stores in the United States have consolidated stores portfolios into a few major store brands. In the deflationary environment of the past two decades, retailers in high-income countries increased their use of technology in supply chain management and built advanced distribution centres with sophisticated material-handling systems to drive efficiency. Wal-Mart alone spent close to US$ 1 billion in technology investments in 1999. This increased spending on technology has generated significant economies of scale for larger retailers and driven up barriers to entry in the retail industry. Economies of scale also exist in procurement. A larger retailer can leverage its buying power against vendors to obtain better pricing and customized services, including customized logistics solutions across borders. The most powerful retailers also require information-sharing services, such as electronic data interchange, advance shipping notices via the Internet and track-and-trace capabilities. They typically prefer delivery to their own distribution centres where goods are consolidated with other products for delivery to their retail stores. Economies of scale can also be achieved in overseas sourcing. For example, retailers can justify sourcing directly with their own procurement arm in Asia rather than going through an agent; they can more efficiently utilize container space rather than leaving shipping containers partially empty; they can leverage insurance costs and financing costs; they can negotiate better prices with factories because they can offer better volume (Mager, 2003). In recent years, large retailers began hiring in-house product development teams and created their private label lines. The elimination of mark-ups by branded vendors more than offsets the small incremental increases in unit product development costs.

Substantial economies of scale and scope in retail operations have fuelled the rise of large global retailers originated from high-income countries.

5.1.1   Increasing retail concentration in advanced economies

Western Europe

In the past two decades, the three largest retail markets in Europe had all experienced consolidation and become highly concentrated. In Germany, Metro acquired AllKauf and Kriegbaum, while Wal-Mart acquired Wertkauf and Interspar. In the United Kingdom, Wal-Mart acquired ASDA, while Morrison's acquired Safeway. In France, Carrefour merged with Promodes. By 2004, the top five companies accounted for 65 per cent, 72 per cent and 57 per cent of the retail markets in Germany, France and UK, respectively (see Table 5.2). Compared to 1999, the United Kingdom saw its top five retailers market share grow by 5 per cent and Germany saw its top five retailers market share grow by 2 per cent (CSFB, July 2005).

Due to the high levels of concentration in the European markets, a series of regulations have been introduced to protect smaller retailers. For example, Germany restricted shop opening hours and prohibited large retailers such as Wal-Mart, Aldi and Lidl from selling certain basic foods below costs; France implemented the Galland Law, which was designed to keep large retailers from having an unfair pricing advantage against small retailers (CSFB, July 2005).

Table 5.2 Retail concentration in Germany, France and the United Kingdom, 2004

Germany		France		United Kingdom	
Top retailers	Market share (%)	Top retailers	Market share (%)	Top retailers	Market share (%)
Metro	16	Carrefour	22	Tesco	20
Rewe	15	Leclerc	14	Sainsbury	11
Edeka	14	ITM	13	Wal-Mart/ ASDA	10
Aldi	11	Casino	12	Morrisons/ Safeway	10
Schwarz	10	Auchan	11	Co-operative	6
Top five total	65	Top five total	72	Top five total	57
Top ten total	83	Top ten total	89	Top ten total	78

Source: CSFB Equity Research, 26 July 2005.

The United States

The United States is the largest retail market in the world, commanding nearly US$ 6 trillion in consumer spending in 1998, or over one-third of the total spending of the world's top 20 retail markets.[40] Although the US retail market has not yet reached the same level of concentration as in Germany, France and the United Kingdom, the country has witnessed massive retail consolidation in the last two decades. Between 1994 and 2005, the largest ten retail M&A deals in the United States all surpassed US$ 1 billion in transaction value and totalled US$ 56 billion.

Most of the largest retail mergers and acquisitions have been concentrated in the department store sector. Demand stagnation and excess capacity in the department store sector necessitated consolidation. Leading department store chains led the consolidation wave by rapidly acquiring store assets across the nation. Since 1983, the top three department stores in the United States, that is, Federated, May and Dillard, have made nine, 20 and 13 acquisitions of other national retail chains, respectively (see Table 5.3). Between 1988 and 2000, the department store sector in the United States grew by only 15.7 per cent, while the top three department stores grew by 116 per cent. Between 1988 and 2000, the shares of the top three companies in the department store sector rose dramatically from 39 per cent to 73 per cent in the United States (see Table 5.4).

Table 5.3 The top ten retail M&As in the United States, 1994–2005

Date	Transaction	Transaction value (US$ billion)
July 1994	Federated/Macy's merger	4.1
August 1995	Federated acquires Broadway	1.6
May 1998	Dillard's acquires Mercantile stores	3.0
July 1998	Proffitt's acquires Saks	2.3
June 2002	Sears acquires Land's End	1.8
June 2004	May acquires Marshall Field's nine Mervyn's stores	3.2
November 2004	K-Mart acquires Sears	10.5
February 2005	Federated acquires May	17.0
March 2005	Global Toys acquires Toys R Us	7.5
May 2005	TPG and Warburg Pincus acquires Neiman Marcus	5.0

Source: CSFB Equity Research, September 2005.

Table 5.4 Increasing concentration in the US department store sector

Company	1988 Sales (US$ billion)	% of Total sales	2000 Sales (US$ billion)	% of Total sales
Federated Dept. Stores	8.3	17	18.4	32
May Dept. Stores	8.3	17	14.5	26
Dillard Dept. Stores	2.6	5	8.6	15
Top three dept. stores	19.2	39	41.5	73
Total dept. stores	48.9	100	56.6	100

Source: Goldman Sachs Investment Research (2003).

Consolidation in the US department store sector culminated in Federated's US$ 17 billion acquisition of May Department Stores Company in February 2005. The combination of the two largest department stores in the United States increased Federated's revenue base from US$ 16 billion to US$ 25 billion and gave it a footprint of 950 department stores operating in 64 of the nation's top 65 markets. As a result of the merger, Federated Department Stores Inc. alone would occupy roughly half of the market share in the US department store sector. According to the company, the transaction would generate total cost synergies of US$ 450 million, resulting from 'consolidation of central functions, division integrations and the adoption of best practices across the combined company'.[41]

Consolidation in the US retail market has also been driven by the growth of mass discount stores. A relatively new retail format, the mass discount store offers a large variety of good quality products at lowest possible prices. Between 1988 and 2000, sales generated by mass discount stores in the United States grew by almost five-fold, from US$ 45 billion to US$ 222 billion. The rapid growth of discount stores reflected economic and social changes in the United States in the past two decades. After the stock market crash of 1987, consumers curbed spending on luxury and branded goods and become more price conscious. Located in suburban areas, mass discount stores also benefited from the de-urbanization of American society in the past two decades.

By 2000, the mass discount store sector had become almost four times as large as the department store sector.

Growth was uneven within the mass discount sector, as the top three stores, Wal-Mart, K-Mart and Target, grew by over 11 times during this 12-year period. In the United States, both Wal-Mart and Target grew organically by building more stores. Between 1988 and 2000, the market share of the top three mass discount chains increased from 36 per cent to 85 per cent (see Table 5.5). During this period, Wal-Mart's growth was astonishing. In 1988, it generated US$ 1.6 billion in total sales and was completely overshadowed by the leading mass discounter at the time, K-Mart; 12 years later, Wal-Mart's domestic operation had grown to US$ 121 billion, dominating the US mass discount sector with a 55 per cent market share.

Table 5.5   Increasing concentration in the US discount store sector

Company	1988 Sales (US$ billion)	% of Total sales	2000 Sales (US$ billion)	% of Total sales
Wal-Mart – USA	1.6	4	121.9	55
K-Mart	13.5	30	37.0	17
Target	1.4	3	29.3	13
Top three discount stores	16.5	36	188.2	85
Total discount stores	45.3	100	222.2	100

Source: Mager (2003).

5.1.2 International expansion of large retailers

In the past two decades, successful retailers in high-income countries have quickly expanded their operations to other countries. By early 2000, the average firm in the world's largest 100 retailers operated in seven countries (Gabel and Bruner, 2003). In addition to overseas sourcing operations, many large retailers have invested heavily in the emerging markets of East Asia, Latin America and eastern Europe through acquisitions, green field investments and/or joint ventures. In entering retail markets of developing countries, international retailers tend to benefit from several significant advantages, including access to low-cost capital, 'best-practice' knowledge in retail operations, depth of human resources and the ability to source supplies globally.

Royal Ahold (Ahold)

Ahold is a Netherlands-based global family of food retail and food service operators that operate under their own brand names. Given the small size of its domestic market, Ahold was one of the first retailers to expand overseas. Since the late 1970s, Ahold has expanded its presence into most of the markets in Europe, the United States, Central and South America, and southeast Asia, mainly in the form of acquisitions (see Table 5.6).

By early 2000s, its various subsidiaries operated a total of 11,535 stores (9,155 in Europe, 1,300 in United States, 976 in Central and South America, and 104 in southeast Asia), generating total revenues of over €56 billion; its operations hired over a quarter of a million employees. Ahold's strategy of running a portfolio of supermarket and food service companies gave its subsidiaries maximum autonomy to cater to local preferences and regulations. However, the company had been unable to leverage the economies of scale in procurement, technology investments and branding across its vast portfolio of retail operations. By 2002, Ahold had been struggling under financial problems due to overexpansion, a confusing operating structure, accounting scandals, and a lack of overall strategy and direction. In that year, Ahold began restructuring its portfolio by selling off investments in emerging markets and non-core operations in the United States. The company moved subsequently towards more centralization in key areas, such as IT platforms and procurement, where economies of scale apply.

Carrefour

Founded in 1959 in Annecy, Haute-Savoie, France, Carrefour is the largest retailer in Europe. Since the early 1970s, Carrefour has brought

Table 5.6 International expansion of Royal Ahold and Carrefour, 1980–2003

Year	Carrefour			Royal Ahold		
	Investments	Country	Target business	Investments	Country	Target business
1981				Giant Food Stores (A)	USA	Supermarket
1982	Carrefour (N)	Argentina	Hypermarket			
1988	Primistères Group (A)		128 supermarkets	Finast (A)	USA	Supermarket
1989	Carrefour (N)	Taiwan, China	Hypermarket			
1990				Albert (N)	Czech Republic	Supermarket
1991	Euromarché (A)	France	Hypermarket	Tops Mkts (A)	USA	Supermarket
	Montlaur (A)	France	Hypermarket			
	Continent (N)	Greece	Hypermarket			
1992				Jerónimo Martins Retail (JV)	Portugal	Supermarket
1993	Carrefour (N)	Italy and Turkey	Hypermarket			
1994	Carrefour (N)	Mexico and Malaysia	Hypermarket	Red Food Stores (A)	USA	55 supermarkets in Tennessee and Georgia
1995	Carrefour (N)	China	Hypermarket	Mayfair (A)	USA	Supermarkets
1996	Carrefour (N)	Thailand, Korea and Hong Kong, China	Hypermarket	Stop & Shop (A)	USA	Supermarket chain in New England
	Félix Potin (A)	France	Convenience store chain			
1997	Carrefour (N)	Singapore and Poland	Hypermarket	Van der Spek (A)	Netherlands	Food supply company
	Catteau (A)	France	Supermarket chain	SuperMar (A)	Brazil	Supermarket

Year	Company	Country		Acquisition	Country	Activity
1998	Comptoir Modernes (C)	France	Hypermarkets	Le Drugstore (A)		Health and beauty care stores
	Carrefour (N)	Chile, Colombia, Indonesia	Hypermarket	Disco (A)	Argentina	Supermarket
				Giant Food (A)	USA	Supermarket
				Santa Isabel (A)	Chile, Peru and Paraguay	Supermarket
1999	Lojas Americanas (A), Planaltao (A), Roncetti (A), Mineirao (A), Rainha (A), Dallas (A) and Continente (A)	Brazil	85 supermarkets	La Fragua (JV)	Guatemala, El Salvador, Honduras	Supermarket
				ICA (JV)	Scandinavia	Supermarket
	Promod (M)	France	Top European food retailing group	Seven Spanish retailers (A)	Spain	150 supermarkets
2000	Maus (JV)	Switzerland	Hypermarket	PYA/Monarch (A)	USA	Food distribution
	GB (C)	Belgium	Food retailing	Boots Stores (A)	Netherlands	Health and beauty care
	Gruppo GS (C)	Italy	Food retailing	Supermercados (A)	Chile	Supermarket
	Carrefour (N)	Japan	Hypermarket	Mea-De Wilde-De Loore (A)	Belgium	Food service
	Marinopoulos (I)	Greece	Hypermarket	Bompre (A)	Brazil	Supermarket
				Sugar Creek (A)	USA	Convenience gas stores
				US FoodService (A)	USA	Food distributor
				Peapod (A)	USA	Internet grocer
				Golden Gallon (A)	USA	Convenience gas stores

Table 5.6 (Continued)

Year	Carrefour			Royal Ahold		
	Investments	Country	Target business	Investments	Country	Target business
2001	Norte (C)	Argentina	Food retailing	Mutual Distributors	USA	Food distributor
	Carrefour (N)	France	Motorway network (17 service stations)	Superdiplo (A)	Spain	Supermarket
				Parkway Food Service (A)	USA	Food distributor
				Amicus Financial (JV)	USA	Financial Svc.
				Dansk Supermarket (JV)	Sweden and Norway	Discount stores and hypermarkets
				Alliant Exchange (A)	USA	Food service
				Bruno's Supermarkets (A)	USA	Food stores
2002				CSU (JV)	Costa Rica	Food stores
				Barbosa (A)	Brazil	Food stores
				Allen Foods (A)	USA	Food svc. distr.
				Lady Baltimore (A)	USA	Food svc. distr.
				Jerónimo Martins (A)	Poland	Hypermarkets
2003	Hyparlo (A)	Italy	Hypermarket			
	Norges Gruppen (JV)	Norway	Hypermarket			
	Anon. (A)	Poland	Two hypermarkets			

Sources: Company annual reports; company websites
Notes: N = new opening; M = merger; A = acquisition; C = controlling stake (over 50 per cent ownership); I = investment less than 50 per cent; JV = joint venture; Anon. = anonymous.

its hypermarket format to retail markets around the world through acquisitions, green field investments and joint ventures (see Table 5.6). Simultaneously, it has built up substantial presence in supermarket, hard discount stores and convenience store formats. By 2004, it had established more than 10,378 stores in 29 countries, generating €89 billion in consolidated sales; its stores hired 420,000 employees. Unlike Ahold, Carrefour's international operations are more centralized, with most of its overseas stores running under the Carrefour brand and with a higher degree of standardization in hypermarket, supermarket, discount and convenience store formats. In many large emerging markets, such as China, Argentina, Brazil and Mexico, Carrefour has been the only worthy opponent to Wal-Mart in the hypermarket space.

Wal-Mart

Wal-Mart first established its international operation in 1991 by entering a joint venture in Mexico. By 2002, Wal-Mart operated 1,212 stores in nine countries outside of the United States and employed more than 300,000 associates.[42] In that year, the international division achieved US$ 41 billion in sales and an operating profit of more than US$ 2 billion[43] (see Table 5.7). If Wal-Mart International were a stand-alone company, it would rank number 33 on 2002's *Fortune* 500 list based on sales.[44]

Wal-Mart's international operations have always been subject to a high degree of control by its headquarters. Questions have been raised

Table 5.7   Wal-Mart's international expansion

Year	Country	Mode of entry	2002–03 units	2002 employees	2002 sales (US$ million)
1991	Mexico	JV	595	93,000	10,980
1992	Puerto Rico	IE	55	8,000	2,000
1994	Canada	A	213	52,000	5,643
1995	Brazil	IE	22	6,000	421
	Argentina	IE	11	4,000	100
1996	China	JV	26	15,000	517
	Indonesia	JV	Exited	NA	NA
1997–98	Germany	A	95	16,000	2,408
1998	South Korea	A	4	3,000	741
1999	United Kingdom	A	229	125,000	17,430
2002	Japan	34% stake holder	400	NA	NA

Source: Ghemawat *et al.* (2004).
Notes: JV = joint venture, IE = internal expansion, A = acquisition.

about whether Wal-Mart's business model is applicable to other markets in the world, where consumer preferences are different. In 1999, Wal-Mart reduced its international division staff at Bentonville by 50 per cent, and gave the individual executives greater decision-making authority, especially in the areas of operations and merchandising. The company set up 'bandwidths of responsibility' that clarified which decisions could be made locally and which should involve Bentonville. It also established certain governance rules for the finance teams in other countries, which were expected to report on progress in the markets. In 2003, Wal-Mart's CEO, Lee Scott, had challenged John Menzer, the newly appointed international division head, to generate one-third of future sales and profit growth from outside of the United States.[45]

5.1.3 Rise of global retail giants

The second half of the twentieth century witnessed the rise of global retail giants such as Wal-Mart, Carrefour and Royal Ahold. As a new modern trade format, the national retail chains in advanced economies grew at the expense of traditional retail channels on the strength of their wide product selections, uniformly low prices, satisfactory product quality, ease of access and pleasant shopping environments. In 1954, there were no retail firms in the *Fortune* 500. In 2003, there were a total of 30 global retailers among the world's 500 largest corporations, accounting for US$ 1.2 trillion in total turnover and employing almost six million workers (*Fortune*, 3 March 2003). All of them were based in developed countries. The largest five retailers, namely Wal-Mart, Carrefour, Royal Ahold, Metro and Kroger, accounted for over half a trillion dollars in sales and employed over 2.6 million workers (see Table 5.8).

At the beginning of the twenty-first century, Wal-Mart surpassed BP to become the largest company in the world in terms of sales and employment. In 2003, the company generated total sales of US$ 263 billion –

Table 5.8   The world's largest retailers, 2003

Company	Country	Revenues (US$ billion)	Employees
Wal-Mart	USA	263	1,500,000
Carrefour	France	80	419,040
Royal Ahold	Netherlands	64	257,140
Metro	Germany	61	198,486
Kroger	USA	54	289,000

Source: *Fortune*, 3 March 2003.

more than the combined sales of the next four retailers, Carrefour, Royal Ahold, Metro, and Kroger. There was speculation that Wal-Mart would reach US$ 1 trillion in sales in just ten years.[46] With 1.5 million employees, Wal-Mart was also the largest private employer in the world. As *Fortune*, which selected Wal-Mart as America's 'Most Admired Company' in 2003, commented, 'the company has created a new definition of bigness'. The magazine compiled a series of statistics to show the truly daunting size of the global giant:

- Wal-Mart's sales on one day in the fall of 2003 – US$ 1.42 billion – were larger than the GDPs of 36 countries.
- It is the biggest employer in 21 US states, with more people in uniform than the US Army.
- It plans to grow [its sales] this year by the equivalent of – take your pick – one Dow Chemical, one PepsiCo, one Microsoft, or one Lockheed Martin.
- If the estimated US$ 2 billion it loses through theft each year were incorporated as a business, it would rank number 694 on the *Fortune* 1,000.[47]

At the end of the twentieth century, the world's largest 100 retailers were all based in high-income countries, and five high-income countries accounted for 84 of the 100 largest retailers in the world.[48] The United States in particular was home to 42 of the world's top 100 retailers, accounting for 46 per cent of retail sales generated by this group.[49]

5.2 Systems integration in the retail industry

As retailers increase in size and footprint, they have been able to use their procurement power to lower merchandising costs. For most vendors, large global and national retail chains have become the largest and most important distribution channel. For example, in 2003, Wal-Mart accounted for between 15 per cent and 30 per cent of the total sales volume of large *Fortune* 500 companies such as Procter & Gamble (P&G), Gillette, Mattel, Kimberly-Clark and Revlon, while none of the vendors accounted for more than 3 per cent of Wal-Mart's sales. When suppliers visit Wal-Mart's headquarters in Bentonville, they are shown into small interview rooms equipped with only a table and four chairs. There, according to observers, the negotiation over terms 'often boiled down to a single price on the invoice'.[50]

Procurement economies constitute only one of the competitive advantages of large retailers. As competitive pressures intensify in global retail markets, the visibility and control over supply chains have become critical competences of large retailers. Over the past two decades, the retailers have increased their integrative functions in the supply chain through supply chain dis-intermediation, use of IT and greater collaboration with top vendors.

Supply chain dis-intermediation

Starting in the early 1990s, large retailers gradually began to bypass manufacturers' representatives, so as to save 3 to 4 per cent on goods formerly sourced through them.[51] Most retailers have built up large in-house global sourcing departments and only use distributors/middlemen when dealing with very small manufacturers, where a direct relationship is not efficient. Wal-Mart, for example, buys 90 per cent of its dollar volume in the United States directly from 3,600 vendors.[52]

Apart from cutting out wholesalers, large retailers have increasingly integrated backwards and begun to develop their own private label products. Most large US retailers have developed their own brands (see Table 5.9).

The trend of private labelling, originally developed in apparel, has now become prevalent in other categories, including home furnishing, personal care, food and beverages, electronics, shoes and toys. In 1994, private label products already accounted for 17.3 per cent of US retail

Table 5.9   Private labels of select large retailers

	Retailer	Private labels
Department stores	Federated/May	Green Dog, Tools of the Trade
	Dillard's	Rowntree & Yorke
	JC Penney	Town-Craft, JC Penney Home Collection, Stafford
	Kohl's	Croft & Barrow
	Nordstrom	BP, Halogen, Caslon, Pure Stuff, Entier, Norsport, Amalfi, John W. Nordstrom
Mass merchants	Wal-Mart	Great Value, Hometrends, Equate, Kids Connection, Ilo, Durabrand, Main Stays
	Target	Merona, Restore & Restyle, Xhilaration, Archer Farms
	Dollar General	Colver Valley, DG Guarantee
	Family Dollar	Field Trail, Cat Cafe

Source: CSFB Equity Research, September 2005.

sales in terms of units, and 12.5 per cent in terms of value; by 2004, these numbers had increased to 19.4 per cent and 15.2 per cent, respectively (CSFB, August 2005). Compared to branded manufacturers, retailers have often been able to offer products at similar quality but substantially lower prices. The growth of private labels has therefore been caused by 'the quality gap between brands and private label being smaller than the price gap' (ibid.). By cutting out the branded supplier, private labelling allows retailers to pass on a large part of the value originally captured by national brands to the consumers without having to compromise their own margins. The retailers' direct involvement in product development and sourcing has given them greater control as well as cost visibility over every segment of the supply chain.

Use of information technology

The application of advanced information technology in retail operations has enhanced sales monitoring, forecasting and planning, as well as supply chain management for large retailers. In order to work more effectively with vendors, Wal-Mart has invested heavily in IT. In the early 1990s, it communicated with 90 per cent of its vendors through its electronic data interchange system, which included forecasting, planning, replenishing and shipping applications. Wal-Mart's *Retail Link* private exchange, which reportedly cost the company US$ 4 billion to develop, provides its vendors with computer access to point-of-sale data on the two-year sales trends and the inventories of their products on a store-by-store basis. By 2002, all of Wal-Mart's suppliers were required to use Retail Link.[53]

Vendor collaboration

Private labelling trends have driven retailers to invest in areas that had traditionally been competences of the vendors. As a result, vendors are now challenged to create more value in the retail supply chain. Today, working with large retailers usually requires much more than just low prices; it requires a great deal of service and management level involvement from the suppliers. For example, in order to work closely with Wal-Mart, more than 450 suppliers have opened Bentonville offices to be near their biggest customer. One such supplier, Newell Rubbermaid, which supplies goods including Rubbermaid plastic containers, Graco baby products and Parker and Waterman pens, built a mini-replica of Wal-Mart's store sections, complete with the same shelving, lighting and fittings. The supplier uses the replica to create the best layout of its products on the retailer's shelves.

Rubbermaid built its Bentonville office 'according to Wal-Mart's Spartan style, down to the carpet'.[54] Procter & Gamble offers a good example of the level of service Wal-Mart gets from its most capable suppliers. In 2003, P&G employed more than 70 people in Bentonville to manage its products for the retailer, including dedicated account managers, outlet representatives, logistics managers, financial analysts and IT personnel. For large national retailers, the most capable vendors were often able to offer highly differentiated service, including frequent store visits by dedicated sales representatives, logistics support, promotion programmes, sharing of category expertise and consumer insights.

Large retailers often seek to build strong collaborative relationships with many of their most important vendors. Every year, each Wal-Mart department develops computerized, strategic business planning packets for its vendors, sharing with them the department's sales, profitability, and inventory targets, macroeconomic and market trends, and Wal-Mart's overall business focus. The packets also specify Wal-Mart's expectations of them, and solicit their recommendations for improving Wal-Mart's performance as well as their own. In addition, Wal-Mart encourages its top 75 suppliers to include it in three-year strategic negotiations involving decisions such as factory size and location.[55] Sam Walton explains the rationale for what he calls a 'partnership model':

> 'in our situation today, we are obsessed with quality as well as price, and, as big as we are, the only way we can possibly get that combination is to sit down with our vendors and work out the costs and margins and plan everything together. By doing that, we give the manufacturer the advantage of know what our needs are going to be a year out, or six months out, or even two years out ... we both win.'[56]

The emergence of 'exclusive national brands' in the US retail market testifies to the increasingly tight collaboration between large retailers and vendors. Under this arrangement, branded manufacturers offer a particular retailer exclusive right of distribution of their products or sub-segments of their core brands (see Table 5.10). For example, Nike has created 'Starter' as a distinctively branded sneaker category exclusively for Wal-Mart. The arrangement usually leverages retailers' formidable in-house sourcing infrastructure to handle all aspects of the production and distribution processes; vendors would therefore focus on product design and branding. For retailers, exclusive access to popular brands increases appeal to their consumers and therefore shop floor traffic. For vendors, the arrangement allows them to differentiate

Table 5.10 Select 'exclusive brand' arrangements

Retailer	Exclusive brands	Vendor
JC Penney	Bisou Bisou Nicole by Nicole Miller	Bisou Bisou Nicole Miller
Kohl's	American Beauty Tony Hawk by Quiksilver Candies Apparel Chaps for women/ children	American Beauty Quiksilver Candies Chaps
Wal-Mart	GE Small Electrics Starter	General Electric Nike
Target	Isaac Mizrahi Cherokee Fieldcrest C9 by Champion Eddie Bauer	Isaac Mizrahi Cherokee Group Fieldcrest Champion Eddie Bauer

Source: CSFB Equity Research, 23 September 2005.

their products and services with retail customers without significant incremental investment.

5.3 Cascade effect

Large corporations have become increasing dominant in the retail space of high-income countries. For example, Wal-Mart's stores now command as much as 30 per cent of the US market in several household staples, such as disposable diapers and shampoo (see Table 5.11). According to *Fortune* (2003), Wal-Mart is not only America's biggest retailer of groceries, but also its biggest seller of DVDs, toys, guns, diamonds, apparel, dog food, detergent, jewellery, sporting goods, video games, socks, bedding, and toothpaste. As the world's largest vendor of DVDs, Wal-Mart is also the largest single revenue generator for Hollywood in the world. Wal-Mart's aggressive expansion plans in the United States could boost the company's share in US food sales and drugstore sales to as much as 35 per cent and 25 per cent, respectively, by 2010.[57]

The dominance of giant retailers has driven the consolidation of their main vendors. As mentioned, suppliers are required to provide increasing services, including information sharing, logistics services

Table 5.11   Wal-Mart's US market share in select merchandise

Product	WaltMart's US market share (%)
Dog food	36
Disposable diapers	32
Photographic film	30
Toothpaste	26
Pain remedies	21
Apparel	13

Source: *Fortune*, March 2003; Goldman Sachs Investment Research.

(e.g., cross-border transportation, warehousing, and customs clearing, and track and trace capabilities), consumer analysis and seasonal and annual planning. In addition, the vendor must offer products that generate a satisfactory rate of stock turnover for the retailer. The requirements have substantially increased the level of investments undertaken by major vendors in IT, logistics, sourcing, branding, and market and consumer analysing, which have erected barriers to entry and increased pressure for consolidation among existing vendors.

5.3.1   Food

Food preparation has been one of mankind's most ancient activities. Since the late nineteenth century, technological progress as well as cultural and lifestyle changes have dramatically changed the way in which inhabitants in industrialized economies cultivate, harvest, transport, prepare, consume, store and dispose of food. One may argue that over the past century, progress in the food system has created more for human welfare than progress in the prior two thousand years (Cotterill, 2000). In advanced economies, this period has seen the development of a science-based, industrial food system, in which large corporations with strong national and international brands emerged and grew. These large corporations are concentrated in the food manufacturing and retailing stages.

Until 1980, branded food manufacturers had dominated the food supply chain. About 80 per cent of all raw food in the United States had to pass through the processing and manufacturing stage (Rogers, 2000). Substantial economies of scale and scope in food procurement, R&D, distribution, and branding have all facilitated the growth of large food manufacturers. Strong R&D capabilities enabled large companies, such as Heinz, Campbell Soup, and General Mills, to play a critical role in the technological development in the food supply chain. In addition, the largest food manufacturers invested heavily not only in market research to understand consumer demands, but also in advertising to create instant brand recognition in national and international markets.

Manufacturers vs. retailers

In the past 25 years, rapidly growing supermarket chains with regional or national coverage challenged for leadership in the food supply chain. While selling products for branded manufacturers, retailers created their own private label offerings by integrating back into food processing. Consolidation in the retail sector of advanced economies has led to large increases in concentration in food retailing. Between 1992 and 1999, the share of the top six supermarket chains of total supermarket sales in the United States increased from 32 per cent to 50 per cent (Cotterill, 2000). At the same time, consumer acceptance of private label food products has increased substantially. In 2004, private label products accounted for about one-third of sales of canned fruit, cheese, and canned vegetables, one quarter of bread sales, and a significant share of ketchup (18 per cent), refrigerated dough (17 per cent), yogurt (14 per cent), luncheon meats (14 per cent), condensed soup (13 per cent), cookies (11 per cent), dry dinner (11 per cent), canned seafood/tuna (10 per cent), toaster pastries (10 per cent) and dog food (10 per cent) in the US retail sector.[58]

In the past two decades, the balance of power in the food system has shifted from branded food manufacturers to retailers. As an important indicator, the relative sizes of the largest firms in the two sectors have changed dramatically. In 1988, the world's largest food and consumer products company was Philip Morris (following its acquisition of Kraft), which generated total sales of US$ 39 billion; the world's largest retailer at the time was K-Mart, which generated total sales of US$ 13.5 billion – one third of the size of Philip Morris. In 2003, the world's largest food company was Nestlé, which generated total sales of US$ 65 billion; in comparison, the world's largest retailer, Wal-Mart, generated total sales of US$ 263 billion – four times the size of the largest food company.

Consolidation of food manufacturers

The growth of private label products effectively drove the commoditization of manufactured and packaged food products. For food manufacturers, the ability to differentiate on quality waned as private labels improved, and maintaining a differentiated brand image became more complex and costly with media fragmentation (CSFB, August 2005).

Since the 1980s, mergers and acquisitions in the food industry in advanced economies have proceeded at a high pace. Every year, the United States witnessed at least 400 cases of mergers and acquisitions in its food industry. During 1997–99, the pace of M&As in the US food industry accelerated to 700–800 cases per year (Rogers, 2000). Large merger and acquisition cases included the Philip Morris US$ 5.6 billion acquisition of General Foods (1985), its US$ 12.9 billion acquisition of Kraft (1988) and Kraft's US$ 15 billion acquisition of Nabisco (2000), ConAgra's acquisition of Hunt-Wesson (1991) and IHP (2000), PepsiCo's acquisition of Tropicana (1998) and Quaker Foods (2001), and General Mill's acquisition of Pillsbury (2000). With the slowing growth of food markets and enormous pressure from large food retailers, the pace of consolidation among food manufacturers continued at a high level in recent years. During 2000–05, the largest seven US packaged food manufacturers alone spent a total of US$ 25 billion in cash acquisitions (see Table 5.12).

Table 5.12 Cash spending on acquisitions by the largest US packaged food manufacturers, 2000–05

	2004–05 sales (US$ billion)	Total cash spent on acquisitions 2000–05 (US$ billion)	Major acquisitions, 2000–05
Kraft	32.5	16.1	Nabisco (2000), Nova Brasilia (2001), Prestige (2001), Samar (2001), Gaouar (2001)
Sara Lee	19.6	3.0	Retail coffee brands from Nestlé (2000), Earthgrains (2001)
ConAgra	14.6	1.2	IHP (2000), Lightlife (2000)
General Mills	11.2	4.3	Pillsbury (2000)
Kellogg	9.6	4.1	Keebler (2001)
Heinz	8.4	1.7	Danone's HP Food Division (2005), HP Sauce (2005), Lea & Perrins (2005)
Campbell Soup	7.5	1.1	Leading instant dry soup and bouillon brands in Europe, including Oxo, Batchelors, Heisse Tasse, Blå Band and Roycoi (2001), Snack Foods Ltd (2002), Erin Food (2002).

Source: Company annual reports and websites.

Focusing on core activities

As the wave of consolidation continued in the food industry, major food manufacturers were focusing on their core competences by streamlining business portfolios. As a CSFB research report remarked, 'While size is important when dealing with a consolidating retail sector...a focus on core strengths often seems a surer path to success' (CSFB, August 2005: 76). In the early 2000s, many top US food manufacturers engaged in business restructurings that allowed them to focus on 'core businesses', which were the top food brands in their respective categories (see Table 5.13). In addition, major food manufacturers were cutting unprofitable product lines to enhance efficiency and profitability. After Hershey reduced its Stock Keeping Units (SKUs) from 2,500 to 1,300, Kraft, Heinz, Campbell Soup, General Mills all announced major SKU cutting programmes.

Emergence of giant global food companies

Merger and acquisition activities have created giant global food companies. In 2004, the world's largest food companies were Nestlé and

Table 5.13 Major restructurings by large US food manufacturers, 2000–05

Company	Major Restructurings
Heinz	In 2002, Heinz sold a number of businesses, including its US StarKist seafood, North American petfoods and pet snacks, US private label soup, College Inn broth, and US baby food businesses to Del Monte Foods Company. In 2005, Heinz again announced plans to divest a number of non-core international operations.
ConAgra Foods	In the early 2000s, ConAgra divested a number of low-margin businesses, including its canned seafood, cream cheese and blue cheese brands, its crop input business, and its chicken business. In 1998, 51 per cent of its sales came from fresh meat and other commodities; by 2004, over 80 per cent of its sales came from branded packaged foods.
Sara Lee	In 2005, Sara Lee began a multi-year plan that would dispose of 40 per cent of the company's revenues, including its apparel, European packaged meats, US retail coffee and direct selling businesses. After the restructuring, Sara Lee will focus on its food, beverage, and household and body care businesses.
Kraft	In 2005, Kraft sold its Lifesavers and Altoids businesses to Wrigley.

Source: Company websites.

Altria, each of which were constructed out of a string of mergers and acquisitions. Nestlé was founded in Switzerland in 1866 and grew to substantial size through mergers with Anglo-Swiss Condensed Milk Co. (1905), Peter, Cailler, Kohler Chocolats Suisses (1929) and Alimentana (1947). The company quickened its pace of acquisition in the past 20 years in order to gain scale and capitalize on globalization opportunities. Major acquisitions included Carnation (1985), Buitoni-Perugina (1988), Rowntree (1988), Perrier (1992), San Pellegrino (1998), Spillers Petfoods (1998), PowerBar (2000), Ralston Purina (2001), Scholler (2002), Chef America (2002), Movenpick (2003), Powwow (2003), Dreyer's (2003), Valio's ice cream activities (2004). By 2004, the company generated global sales of CHF 87 billion (US$ 66 billion), and employed 247,000 workers in 470 factories around the world. It manufactures branded products in major food and beverage segments ranging from coffee, water, ice cream, nutrition products, soup, frozen foods, chocolate to food services and pet care. In 2006, the company has 'factories or operations in almost every country in the world' (Nestlé website).

The Altria Group was created in 2002 to hold the food and tobacco businesses of Philip Morris Companies. Philip Morris' food business was built out of large acquisitions that leveraged the company's rich cash flows from cigarette sales. In the past two decades, Philip Morris acquired already large food companies, such as General Foods (1985), Kraft (1988), and Nabisco (2000). In 2004, Kraft Foods, which was restructured to operate most of Altria's food business, generated US$ 32 billion in revenues. Kraft employed 98,000 workers in 70 countries and operated 192 manufacturing and processing facilities around the world. The company ran four global research centres, three in the United States and one in the United Kingdom. It amassed one of the strongest brand portfolios of any packaged goods company, with more than 50 brands valued above US$ 100 million and five brands valued above US$ 1 billion. Its top global brands included Kraft (the world's number one cheese brand), Philadelphia (the world's number one cream cheese brand), Jacobs (coffee), Maxwell House (coffee), Toblerone (chocolates), Oreo (cookies), Ritz (crackers) and Crystal Light/Clight/Tang (beverages).

Increased concentration

Merger and acquisition activities have led to increasing concentration in the food processing and manufacturing industry. In 1995, there were still roughly 16,000 companies involved in food processing in the United States. However, the largest 100 food and tobacco processors accounted for nearly 80 per cent of the value-added, almost doubling their share since 1954. In 1992, these 100 firms accounted for 45 per cent of the total workforce, 50 per cent of the payroll, and 96.4 per cent of media advertising in the US food industry. Within the 100 largest firms, the top 20 took up over 50 per cent of total value-added of the group. The top eight firms alone accounted for 51 per cent of the industry's media advertising spending in 1992, compared to 30 per cent in 1967 (Rogers, 2000). By the end of the twentieth century, the US food industry had segmented into a bi-polar structure, 'where extremely large firms control leading positions in most markets and smaller companies, including start-ups, operate in a competitive fringe trying to serve a particular market niche or develop a new idea. The large companies know that if a new idea turns promising they can buy the entire company after the start-up has borne much of the risk' (ibid.: 8). According to Rogers' study, of the companies in the US food industry (defined by Census bureau's 4-digit SIC code), the food and tobacco processing sector had 53 such industries in 1992, by which date most of which had become oligopolies. The 4-firm concentration ratio in these industries increased on average from 43.9 in 1967 to 53.3 in 1992.

When particular food categories are examined, the level of concentration in US markets is even higher. In food categories such as bacon, cereal, ketchup, chocolate, cookies, soup and yoghurt, the top 2–5 firms accounted for 60–90 per cent of the national market share in 2004 (see Table 5.14).

Table 5.14 US market share of top food manufacturers by category

Category	No. of top players	US market share (%)	Category	No. of top players	US market share (%)
Bacon	Top 5	61	Frozen dinners	Top 3	58
Cat Food	Top 4	83	Frozen pizza	Top 4	81
Ketchup	Top 3	81	Gum	Top 2	91
Cereal	Top 5	90	Luncheon meats	Top 4	53
Chocolate	Top 3	76	Salad dressing	Top 3	61
Coffee	Top 3	76	Snack bars	Top 4	57
Cookies	Top 3	60	Seafood/tuna	Top 3	86
Crackers	Top 3	84	Condensed soup	Top firm	85
Dog food	Top 4	86	RTS soup	Top 2	79
Dough	Top 2	82	Toaster pastries	Top 2	87
Dry dinner	Top 4	82	Yoghurt	Top 2	69

Source: Data complied from *Food Investors' Handbook*, CSFB, August 2005.
Note: Data exclude Wal-Mart sales.

Changes in the structure of food supply chain

Supply chain integration capabilities have become a core competitive competence for food manufacturers and retailers alike. Control over the supply chain affects not only costs, but also food quality as well as the ability to respond to market changes. Instead of buying agricultural produce in agricultural markets, retailers and food processors now increasingly contract directly for much of the produce they sell. An extreme example is the chicken processors in the United States, who have been fully integrated from the hatchery to the processing plants: they hire contract growers to raise chicken to market weight, and supply their own feed and inputs (Rogers, 2000). It is often the case that direct contracts or strategic alliances exist between major growers, processors and retailers. Such relationships lower risks for farmers and assured processors of supplies with required quality and features.

Through direct procurement, food processors/manufacturers and retailers have significantly affected the structure of their supply chain. Retailers and manufacturers often buy directly from a handful of large regional or national suppliers, who can produce according to the formers' stringent quality standards and still offer the best price. For example, Wal-Mart stores in New England only carry Purdue fresh chicken, only Tyson frozen chicken, and only Smithfield fresh pork (Cotterill, 2000). By 'picking the winners' in each food category, Wal-Mart's procurement strategy forecloses the market in these categories to save on trade and marketing expenses for these suppliers, most of which get passed along to consumers as savings. The Purdue's, Tyson's and Smithfield's among the food processors, in turn adopt a similar strategy with *their* suppliers in the tightly coordinated supply chain.

Supply chain coordination by retailers and processors results in increasing concentration in all stages of the food system. Not only has concentration increased at the processing level, but also at the grower level as well. Changes in the structure of the pork supply chain in the United States offers a good example. According to a study by Paarlberg and Haley (2000), between 1985 and 1997, the 4-firm concentration ratio in the American swine packing industry increased dramatically from 32.2 to 54.3, while concentration ratio at the 8-firm level increased from 50.8 to 75.7. During this period, the number of hog slaughter firms declined almost by one half, from 338 to 184, while the number of plants fell from 403 to 218. Decline was more rapid for smaller firms. Previously, most of the packing firms purchased hogs from growers for cash in local markets. Today, most of the slaughter firms have formed some type of arrangements with specific packers. Roughly two-thirds of animals slaughtered in the United States are estimated to be either directly owned by meat packers or sold under contract.

The changes in procurement method of the meat packers had a substantial impact on hog growers. Between 1980 and 1999, the number of establishments raising hogs in the United States fell from 666,500 to 98,460. Among the growers, increased specialization and scale were dominant trends. The Midwestern states in the United States tended to specialize in grower-finishing tasks due to feed supply proximity and excess shackle space, while neighbouring states tended to focus on gestation and farrowing. At the same time, the scale of hog-growing has increased substantially. By 1995, 2,000 head operations represented 2 per cent of hog growers and 37 per cent of the inventory. Between 1985 and 1999, the number of small hog growers in the United States fell by over 50 per cent.[59]

Growing concentration at the retailing and processing levels of the food supply chain has caused much anxiety among farmers in advanced economies, who worry about loss of bargaining power, negotiating against giant purchasers of their produce. In the United States, farmers often formed cooperatives and bargaining associations in order to improve their bargaining position with large corporate buyers. In many instances, the cooperatives have integrated forward by creating and marketing their own brands, such as Sun Maid Raisins, Sunkist Oranges, Ocean Spray Cranberries, Welches Grape Juice, Land O'Lakes Butter (Cotterill, 2000). By 1987, the largest 100 cooperatives had controlled 63 per cent of the shipments in the butter market and 44 per cent of the shipments in the rice milling market in the United States.

5.3.2 Consumer products

The most prominent consolidation activity in the vendor space so far is Procter & Gamble's US$ 57 billion acquisition of Gillette, the world's leading maker of men's shaving supplies as well as the maker of Duracell batteries, in January 2005. The primary motive of the acquisition was scale, as the deal would give P&G more control over shelf space at the nation's retailers and grocers. 'Shelf space is diamond-encrusted gold. It's exposure to the consumer and everyone wants exposure to the consumer', said retail analyst Kurt Barnard, 'They each had a lot of economic power before, but with the marriage they'll have a lot more power, power to get shelf space, preferred positions, all of that' (CNNMoney, 28 January 2005). James Kilts, CEO of Gillette, confirmed the importance of scale behind the acquisition, 'I am a great believer in scale...we believe we can bring these companies together and create a juggernaut'. The combined company would have total revenues of close to US$ 70 billion with annual advertising spending between US$ 6–7 billion. P&G has 16 products that have sales of more than US$ 1 billion each, and Gillette has another five. The increase in size and the companies' expanded portfolio of must-have brands would allow the new P&G to gain greater leverage against retail giants such as Wal-Mart and Costco, as well as with media companies in advertising procurement. It is no coincidence that Wal-Mart was the largest customer for both P&G and Gillette, accounting for 17 per cent and 13 per cent of their annual sales, respectively (see Table 5.15).

Kilts believed that due to the enormous pressure from large retailers, the consumer products industry would eventually undergo further consolidation: 'I believe the consumer product industry needs to consolidate...I'd rather lead than end up with the leftovers' (*Billings Gazette*, 29 January 2005). Kilts' remarks came at a time when many segments of the US consumer product industry were already highly concentrated. For example, five companies control over 85 per cent of the US$ 1.3 billion US toothpaste market, with the two leading brands, Colgate and Crest, accounting for over 60 per cent of the market. Just three companies, P&G, Unilever and Church & Dwight, control 77 per cent of the US$ 2 billion US detergent market. Three companies, Nike, Adidas and Reebok, almost entirely dominate the sale of basketball sneakers in the United States. Just two companies, Phillip Morris and RJ Reynolds, control 72 per cent of US cigarette sales; with the next two companies, Lorrillard and Brown & Williamson, the top four companies

Table 5.15   Profiles of P&G and Gillette, 2004

	P&G	Gillette
Revenues	US$ 54 billion	US$ 14 billion
Advertising spend	US$ 5.5 billion	US$ 1 billion
Market capitalization	US$ 141 billion	US$ 45 billion
Employment	110,000	29,400
Product lines	Fabric and home care, baby care, beauty care, healthcare, snacks and beverages	Blades and razors, batteries (Duracell), oral care, automatic razors (Braun), personal care
Largest customer	Wal-Mart (17% of sales)	Wal-Mart (14% of sales)

Source: Company annual reports, Yahoo!Finance.

Table 5.16 Concentration in select US consumer product categories

Category	Top companies	Collective share (%)	Source
Toothpaste	Colgate-Palmolive, P&G, GlaxoSmithKline, Unilever, Church & Dwight	85	www.AdAge.com
Detergent	P&G, Unilever, Church & Dwight	77	www.AdAge.com
Basketball sneakers	Nike, Adidas, Reebok	95	www.oligopolywatch.com
Cigarettes	Phillip Morris, RJ Reynolds	72	IRI Capstone
Fashion dolls	Mattel	60	*Gazette Times*, 22 February 2005

control over 90 per cent of the US cigarette market. Mattel, creator of the Barbie doll series, sells 60 per cent of the fashion dolls in the United States. P&G's acquisition of Gillette shows that stringent requirements from large retailers are pressuring the consumer products industry in high-income countries to consolidate even further (see Table 5.16).

5.3.3 Apparel

The trend of vendor consolidation is apparent in the 'better priced' segment[60] of the apparel industry, where the most capable companies with strong product, sourcing and logistics skills gained market share from smaller, less capable competitors. At the same time, larger vendors with stronger brand equity and financing capabilities have been acquiring other brands. Two of the most acquisitive wholesale apparel companies in the United States are Liz Claiborne and Jones Apparel Group, with each company operating a portfolio of more than 20 brands. They have targeted companies that offer growth and help diversify them away from better women's sportswear in department stores where they already hold dominant positions. The 'mega brand' strategy, where branded apparel vendors put different brands under one roof, allows vendors to maximize their operating efficiency by putting more volume passing through the same sourcing and logistics system. It allows the vendors to achieve economies of scale in their investments in IT, logistics and sourcing capabilities. In 2002, Liz Claiborne was able to source

Table 5.17 Top vendor share in US department store apparel sales, 2002

Brand	Market share total (%)	Market share men's (%)	Market share women's (%)
Jones Apparel	22	8	30
Liz Claiborne	22	5	31
Tommy Hilfiger	12	16	10
Ralph Lauren	11	30	0
Warnaco	11	8	12
Nautica	7	16	2
Total top six	84	83	84

Source: Mager (2003).

180 million units of apparel in 45,000 styles from 300 factories in 30 countries through its massive international sourcing system.

In 2002, the top six brands controlled 84 per cent market share in the premium department store channel of distribution in the United States. In the 'better priced' women's apparel category, the top two brands controlled over 60 per cent of the market share in department stores. In the 'better priced' men's apparel category, the top three brands controlled over 61 per cent of the market share in department stores (see Table 5.17).

5.4 Summary

Despite the strong local characteristics of retail operations, economies of scale and scope in procurement, branding, product development and technology investments have driven the consolidation of retail industries in advanced economies. Through rapid expansion and mergers and acquisitions, large global retailers have emerged to occupy significant shares of consumer spending in almost every major retail market. At the same time, these large retailers have tightened their control over the retail supply chain through supply chain dis-intermediation, the use of information technology, and closer vendor collaborations. In many aspects, the retail–vendor relationship has transcended the simple price relationship. The supermarket or the department store is no longer a 'free market' in which buyers and sellers deal at arm's length. Instead, substantial planning and coordination exist between retailers and their most important vendors. These activities have drastically increased the efficiencies of the retail supply chain and created innovations such as exclusive brands.

For vendors, retailers' enormous procurement power and their integrative activities have created significant pressure for consolidation. In many sectors, especially food, the pressure for consolidation has cascaded down from food manufacturers and processors to farmers and growers at the bottom of the supply chain, causing increasing concentration at almost every stage of the value chain.

6
Implications for Firm-level Catch-Up in Developing Countries

6.1 Competition, industrial concentration and technical progress

The period since the 1970s has seen a large change in the nature of business organization, amounting to nothing less than a 'business revolution'. As global markets have opened up, multinational companies typically have responded by divesting their 'non-core' businesses to focus on a small array of closely related products in which they have global leadership, achieved through the possession of a combination of superior brand and technology, and through economies of scale and scope in both areas. The large size and business focus of leading firms has enabled them to benefit greatly from economies of scale in procurement. Leading global firms have increasingly outsourced manufacturing and 'non-core' service functions, to focus on the 'brain' functions of design, product development, final assembly, marketing and financing. Alongside the growth of outsourcing, they have also developed skills in systems integration and coordination of their supply chain. Leading global firms have also been able to attract the best employees in the international 'battle for talent'.

In almost every sector, the period since the 1970s has seen an unprecedented level of mergers, acquisitions and divestment, with leading firms using this to consolidate their position at the centre of global markets by achieving focus and scale. In addition to highly publicized large-scale mergers there has been a continuous process of smaller scale acquisitions, with leading companies each acquiring numerous small and medium-sized firms annually in order to enhance their leading positions in their respective markets.

Levels of global industrial consolidation within each sector have advanced remorselessly. The process has affected almost every sector, from the world's most sophisticated, high-technology capital goods, to the simplest consumer goods. It is as though a law has come into play, under which in every sector, the top half dozen systems integrator firms, with superior brands and/or technologies account for over one half of the entire global market in the particular product. This is the case in industries as diverse as large commercial airliners, automobiles, gas turbines, farm equipment, lifts, construction equipment, chemicals, pharmaceuticals, consumer electronics, telecommunications equipment, servers, semiconductors, digital cameras, personal computers, IT software, carbonated soft drinks, salty snacks, beer, confectionary, ice cream, hair colourants, camera film, cigarettes, recorded music, media and marketing, investment banking, accountancy, foreign exchange trading, and water management, Moreover, in different sub-categories within each broad product category, levels of industrial concentration are typically even higher.[61] These dramatic developments are consistent with the persistence in most sectors of a large number of small and medium sized firms, which produce mainly non-branded, low-technology products, supplying local markets, and which collectively occupy a small share of total global markets. These parts of the segmented industrial structure typically supply the lower groups within each country's income distribution.

The explosive advance in industrial consolidation among system integrator firms has produced a powerful consequential impact on industrial structure, which has been termed the 'cascade effect' (Nolan, 2001a). The global industry leaders in each sector have used their procurement power to exert intense pressure on their supply chains, typically requiring leading firms in the upper tiers of the supply chain to supply inputs on a 'just-in-time' basis to production sites around the world. This has intensified the pressure upon supplier firms to build global networks to feed the needs of global customers. The leading systems integrators place intense pressure on their suppliers to achieve technical progress in order to supply inputs of improving technical quality so that they can meet the demands of final customers. Moreover, they exert remorseless pressure on their suppliers to lower prices for a given product quality. This has, in turn, resulted in intense pressure upon supplier firms themselves to merge and acquire, and to divest non-core business, in order to gain scale and focus, enabling them to achieve economies of scale in research and development, procurement, human resources, and subsystems integration.

The impact of this process upon technical progress has been striking. The world's R&D expenditure is highly concentrated. In 2003, the top 700 firms between them spent US$ 366 billion on R&D, an average of US$ 522 million per firm (see Table 6.1). These firms constitute the core of global technical progress. Between them they had revenue of US$ 8,806 billion, constituting the core of the whole global economy. A negligible number of these firms are from developing countries.[62] Even within the top 700 firms, there is a high degree of concentration in R&D expenditure. In 2003, the top 300 firms together spent US$ 291 billion on R&D, accounting for 80 per cent of the world total for the top 700 firms. The top 33 firms, with an R&D expenditure of over US$ 3 billion each, spent a total of US$ 147 billion on R&D, accounting for 40 per cent of the total for the top 700 firms. Between 1995 and 2002, the R&D expenditure of the top 300 firms rose by almost two-thirds, from US$ 177 billion to US$ 291 billion, a growth rate of more than 7 per cent per annum (*FT*, 25 June 1999, and 15 September 2003).

The increased focus on core business among the world's leading systems integrators and subsystems integrators has enhanced the effectiveness of R&D expenditure, allowing benefits from economies of scale and scope. Technical progress in the instruments of R&D, especially IT hardware and software, has further enhanced the effectiveness of R&D spending. In addition, the world's leading firms are rapidly increasing their R&D bases in low and middle income countries, which enables them to obtain greater amounts of knowledge per dollar spent on R&D.

Meaningful measurement of technical progress has eluded economists.[63] The pace of technical progress during the epoch of the global business revolution cannot be unambiguously compared with previous

Table 6.1   The world's top 700 firms by research and development expenditure, 2003

	Total (US$ billion)	Average (mean) R&D expenditure per firm (US$ million)	Share of total (%)
Top 17[(a)]	66	6,000	25
Top 33[(b)]	147	4,500	40
Top 300	291	970	80
Next 400	75	188	20
Top 700	366	522	100

Source: FT, 25 October 2004.
Notes: [(a)] firms with over US$ 4 billion in expenditure on R&D; [(b)] firms with over US$ 3 billion in expenditure on R&D.

periods of rapid technical progress. However, it is self-evident that the period has seen one of the fastest periods of technical progress in human history, led by the oligopolistic firms that dominate the apex of global supply chains, which have in turn powerfully stimulated technical progress at lower levels in the supply chain. We examine briefly technical progress in four sectors in the past two decades.

The IT revolution has been at the heart of technical progress in all sectors. The IT hardware and software sector is by far the most important in terms of global technical progress. In 2003, 180 of the world's top 700 firms by R&D spending were from this sector, accounting for 26 per cent of the total spending on R&D by the world's top 700 companies (DTI, 2004). In 2003, IT hardware and software firms within the top 700 companies together spent US$ 94 billion on R&D, and had combined revenues of US$ 966 billion (*FT*, 25 October 2004). Within these, a group of 22 information technology companies (each with spending of more than US$ 1 billion) spent a total of US$ 62 billion on R&D, which amounted to 66 per cent of the total spending on R&D by the 180 IT firms among the world's top 700 companies (*FT*, 25 October 2004; DTI, 2004).

The massive spending of the world's leading IT companies over the past two decades has stimulated a revolution in information generation and transmission. The revolution in IT has transformed both the nature of capital goods and the nature of a large fraction of final consumption. Goods and services in almost every sector have been comprehensively changed by this technical revolution, from complex engineering products, including aeroplanes, automobiles, farm equipment, and all types of manufacturing machinery, to almost every imaginable service, including mass media, retail, banking, insurance, tourism, transport, and marketing. The IT revolution has universally lowered costs and prices of IT goods and services. It has allowed a dramatic fall in the cost of global communications, transformed the cost and nature of R&D, and facilitated the profound change in the nature of the global firm and its relationship to the surrounding value chain.

However, the epoch of the global business revolution has witnessed dramatic changes in technology in almost every sector. For example, in the automobile industry, both passenger and commercial vehicles have altered radically, with huge reductions in weight, due mainly to advances in technologies embodied in steel, aluminium and plastics; large increases in fuel economy, due both to weight reduction and advances in engine technologies; large increases in vehicle safety, comfort, ease of use, reliability and longevity; and large reduction in polluting emissions.

In the aerospace industry, enormous changes have taken place in the nature of passenger aircraft. Large weight reductions per passenger carried have taken place due to advances in aircraft design, through improvements in each type of construction material, and through increased use of composite materials; large advances have taken place due to continuous progress in engine technologies, including weight reduction, increased fuel efficiency, reduced engine noise, increased engine reliability, and advances in ease of engine maintenance; and large advances have taken place in aircraft safety, due to advances in avionics and flight control systems, and advances in the design and reliability of aircraft components, including seats, engines, landing gear, avionics, and tyres.

In the beverage industry, including both soft drinks and beer, quite limited changes have taken place in the nature of the product, but enormous technical progress has taken place in the nature of the processes involved in producing and distributing beverages. Filling machinery has greatly increased in speed, reliability, and fuel efficiency, alongside reductions in variability of filling height and bottle damage. Packaging technologies have altered radically. Metal cans and PET bottles have joined glass bottles to constitute the three main forms of primary packaging. Introduction of metal cans and PET allowed enormous changes in the appearance of primary packaging, increasing customer satisfaction through increased ease of use and attractiveness of designs. Improved packaging technologies have increased longevity of beverages at peak condition.

All three types of primary packaging have achieved large reductions in package weight, which economizes on use of raw materials, reduces weight in transport and improves ease of use by the final customer. These advances have occurred through intense interaction between leading beverage companies and the suppliers of packaging materials (including steel, aluminium, PET and glass), as well as with the firms that make machinery to produce primary packaging. Large advances have taken place in the machine building industry to produce 'PET preforms', PET blowing equipment, can-making machinery and glass bottle machinery. They have increased speed and reliability, reduced raw material and fuel consumption per unit, and improved packaging design capabilities. Distribution of beverages is enormously intensive in the use of road transport. Improvements in commercial vehicle technologies have greatly increased fuel efficiency in the distribution of beverages.

As these examples indicate, increased focus on core business and increased firm size among both systems integrators and suppliers has increased economies of scale and scope at every level in the value chain. This applies to almost every sector. Alongside dramatic advances in product and process technologies, there has taken place a near universal decline in unit costs and advance in product quality. The epoch of the global business revolution has seen a dramatic rise in levels of industrial concentration. Oligopolistic competition has penetrated almost every level of the supply chain, from the systems integrators downwards, and has been stimulated by intense pressure from the top of the supply chain 'cascading' down through the whole system. Instead of the technical stagnation and real price increase that were predicted by most economists, both 'radical' and mainstream, the epoch has witnessed intense oligopolistic competition, which has been responsible for this epoch's extraordinary technological dynamism. This reality has hardly begun to be absorbed and analysed by economists.[64] For Marx or Schumpeter, the nature and consequences of the global business revolution would be unsurprising.

6.2   Challenges of the global business revolution

The global business revolution, a transformation at the 'core' of the global business system, has profound implications for firms at the 'periphery', which includes firms from developing countries looking to participate in the global economy. It has fundamentally changed how businesses are conducted in the global economy. For a long time, many economists and politicians have advocated 'free trade' as the major means by which firms from developing countries can participate in the global economy. This concept of 'free trade' has often been proffered to developing countries together with the concept of the 'free market', which implies a global market structure in which many firms buy and sell from one another at arms length, competing for shares in a vast market.

Mainstream, neo-classical economists consider that opening up developing economies to global competition provides broad opportunities for indigenous firms to catch up with firms headquartered in the high-income countries. Their view is based on the belief that the basic tendency of capitalism is competition with strict limits to growth of firm size: they believe that by forcing weak firms to compete with strong ones, the weak can learn from the strong, imitate them and overtake them.

The reality of global business today, however, is far from the elegant model of perfect competition assumed in neo-classical theory. In fact, the epoch of the global business revolution since the 1980s has witnessed an unprecedented degree of industrial consolidation and concentration of business power at a global level. The 'commanding heights' of the global business system are almost entirely occupied by firms from high-income countries. This presents a deep challenge for firms and policy makers from developing countries.

6.2.1 Unequal regional distribution of large capable firms

Statistics show great disparity in the regional distribution of firms that lead the global business revolution (see Table 6.2). The high-income economies contain just 15 per cent of the world's total population. Firms headquartered in these countries account for 94 per cent of the companies listed in the *Fortune* 500, which ranks firms by sales revenue. They account for 96 per cent of the firms in the *FT* 500 list of the world's leading firms, ranked by market capitalization. According to the UK Department of Trade and Industry, firms headquartered in high-income countries account for almost 100 per cent of the firms included in the list of the world's top 700 firms ranked by expenditure on research and development, which is a critical indicator of the distribution of global business power and capabilities.

If one takes a closer look at the few large firms from low-income countries, almost all are either in resource sectors or state-owned monopolies; and very often, they are both. Among the Global *Fortune* 500 companies in 2003, 28 firms are from less-developed countries. Their combined revenues account for 3.7 per cent of the total revenues of the *Fortune* 500. Fourteen are from China, four from India, three from Brazil, three from Russia, and one each from Malaysia, Thailand, Mexico, and Venezuela. Among these companies, 12 are state-owned oil and gas companies, six are state-owned banks or insurance companies, and three are telecommunications and utilities companies (see Table 6.3). Due to inherent problems in state ownership and licensed monopolies, size in these cases is rarely a good indicator of business capabilities.

Studying the business capabilities of firms directly, one would find that the ability to drive technology change differed significantly across firms from high- and low-income countries. At the end of the twentieth century, 90 per cent of all R&D spending is concentrated in seven high-income countries, with the United States alone accounting for 40 per cent (Gabel and Bruner, 2003). In 2003, the United States spent a total of US$ 253 billion in R&D activities, with corporations, universities and the Federal government accounting for 68 per cent, 14 per cent, and 9 per cent of the investments, respectively. Large global companies based in advanced countries dominated corporate R&D funding. In 2003, the

Table 6.2 Dominance of the global business revolution by firms based in high-income countries

	Population (2000)		GNP (2000)[a]		GNP (2000)[b]		Fortune 500 companies (2003)[c]		FT 500 companies (2003)[d]		Top 700 companies by R&D spend (2002–03)	
	billion	%	US$ billion	%	US$ billion	%	No	%	No	%	No	%
HIEs	903	15	24,828	80	24,781	55	472	94	480	96	697	100
L/MIEs	5,152	85	6,336	20	20,056	45	28[e]	6	20[f]	4	3	negl.

Sources: FT, 27 May 2004; World Bank, 1998, 2002; *Fortune*, 26 July 2004; DTI, 2003.
Notes: HIEs = high-income economies; L/MIEs = low/middle income economies; [a] at official rate of exchange; [b] at PPP dollars; [c] ranked by sales revenue; [d] ranked by market capitalization; [e] China = 14, India = 4, Brazil = 3, Russia = 3, Mexico = 1, Malaysia = 1, Venezuela = 1, Thailand = 1; [f] Russia = 7, China = 4, India = 3, Mexico = 3, Brazil = 2, India = 1.

Table 6.3   Large companies from low-income countries

Company	Country	Sales (2003) US$ billion	Sector
State Grid	China	58	Utility
Pemex	Mexico	49	Oil and gas
CNPC	China	47	Oil and gas
PDVSA	Venezuela	46	Oil and gas
Petrobras	Brazil	31	Oil and gas
Gazprom	Russia	28	Oil and has
Petronas	Malaysia	26	Oil and gas
Indian Oil	India	25	Oil and gas
China Life	China	21	Finance
China Mobile	China	21	Telecom
ICBC	China	20	Finance
China Telecom	China	19	Telecom
Sinochem	China	19	Petrochemicals
China Construction Bank	China	16	Finance
Yukos	Russia	15	Oil and gas
Banco Do Brasil	Brazil	15	Finance
Cathay Life	China (Taiwan)	14	Finance
Agricultural Bank of China	China	13	Finance
COFCO	China	13	Food
Bharat Petroleum	India	12	Oil and gas
PTT	Thailand	12	Oil and gas
Shanghai Automotive	China	12	Automobile
Hindustan Petroleum	India	12	Oil and gas
Total		544	

Source: *Fortune*, 26 July 2004.

top five US corporations alone spent US$ 33.6 billion on R&D, more than the entire Federal R&D budget (*Technology Review*, December 2004). Small industrial countries had an even greater concentration: during the 1980s, three firms accounted for 81 per cent of Switzerland's R&D. M&A activities since then have resulted in an even more intense concentration of R&D in the hands of few large corporations (Gabel and Bruner, 2003). The ability to invest in product and process innovation by large global firms has dramatically increased the barriers to entry in their respective industries.

However, research and development spending by firms from developing countries has been low and infrequent. For example, in 2003, only 30 per cent of China's large and medium companies engaged in any R&D activities at all; only 25 per cent of China's large and medium

Table 6.4 Distribution of the world's top 320 companies in R&D spending

Country/region	No. of firms	US$ billion spent	% total	Top five firms (US$)
USA	166	120	44	Ford (7.7 billion); GM (5.8 billion); Pfizer (5.1 billion); IBM (4.7 billion); Microsoft (4.3 billion)
Japan	78	66	24	Toyota (5.6 billion); Matsushita (4.6 billion); Sony (3.7 billion); Honda (3.6 billion); NTT (3.3 billion)
EU	68	84	31	DaimlerChrysler (6.4 billion); Siemens (6.2 billion); Glaxo (4.6 billion); Aventis (3.6 billion); Ericsson (3.4 billion)
Developing countries	4	1	0.3	Elan – Ireland (397 million); United Microelectronics – Taiwan, China (213 million); Winbond Electronics – Taiwan, China (170 million); Mosel Vitelic – Taiwan, China (154 million)
Total top 320 firms[a]	320	274	100	

Source: Standard & Poor's.
Note: [a] four firms from Canada – Nortel (US$ 2.3 billion), Bioval (US$ 233 million), Bombardier (US$ 191 million), and ATI Technologies (US$ 172 million), not listed for the purpose of presentation.

companies had established formal R&D institutions (Zhen, 2004). The average R&D expenditure as a percentage of sales among Chinese firms was 0.75 per cent, compared to an average above 3 per cent among Western firms (ibid.).

The ability to create and sustain global brands also differed among firms from high- and low-income countries. The list of the top 100 brands was completely occupied by firms from advanced countries: the United States had 62 of the world's top 100 brands, compared with 30 in the EU, seven in Japan, and one in Korea. There is not a single firm from the low/middle income countries in the list of the world's 'top 100 brands' (Sorrell, 2005). Meanwhile, powerful brands, such as Coca-Cola, have successfully penetrated markets in the developing world, replacing local competitors as the trusted products or services for

Table 6.5   Distribution of the world's top 100 brands, 2003

Country/ region	No. of brands among the global 100 brands	Value of top brands (US$ billion)	% of total	Top five brands
USA	62	705	72	Coca-Cola, Microsoft, IBM, GE, Intel
Europe[a]	30	187	19	Nokia, Mercedes, BMW, Nescafé, SAP
Japan	7	71	7	Toyota, Honda, Sony, Nintendo, Canon
Korea	1	11	1	Samsung
Total global	100	974	100	Coca-Cola, Microsoft, IBM, GE, Intel

Source: *Business Week*, 4 August 2003.
Note: [a] Includes Finland, Germany, Switzerland, United Kingdom, Sweden, France, Italy, Netherlands.

consumers and businesses alike. The enormous economies of scale in global branding has erected significant barriers to entry for latecomers.

6.2.2   Difficulties of 'catch-up'

As the process of globalization continues, firms in low-income countries are increasingly finding themselves either competing with and/or working for multinational firms. As competitors, most of them tend to find that the 'global playing field' is far from being 'level' due to the drastic differences in scale and capabilities. In all three cases examined in this book, industry competition at the global level has been dominated by a few giant firms benefiting from formidable economies of scale and scope in a wide range of value chain activities. The enormous advantages and market dominance of these global giants pose significant challenges for firms from low-income countries to 'catch-up'. Morgan Stanley (1998) estimated that the average sustainability of competitive edge (defined as the number of years it would take an aggressive and well-financed competitor to establish a similar business) to be as long as 23 years for aerospace firms, 14 years for consumer goods firms, and seven years for retail firms. It also estimated the sustainability of competitive edge for Coca-Cola to be over 20 years. For firms from developing countries, catching up with the global giants in this competitive environment seems to be nearly impossible.

However, the challenge is even deeper than it at first appears. The most easily visible part of the structure of industrial concentration is the well-known firms with powerful, globally recognized technologies and/or brands. These constitute the 'systems integrators' or 'organizing brains' at the apex of extended value chains. As they have consolidated their leading positions, they have exerted intense pressure across the whole supply chain in order to minimize costs and stimulate technical progress. This book has closely examined the value chain structures in three sectors with totally different products and services, aerospace, beverages and retail. It has shown that these sectors have striking similarities in the way in which the core systems integrators have stimulated a comprehensive transformation of industrial structure across the whole supply chain. At every level there has taken place an intense process of industrial concentration, mainly through merger and acquisition, as firms struggle to meet the strict requirements that are the condition of their participation in the systems integrators' supply chains.

This 'cascade effect' has profound implications for the nature of competition. It means that the challenge facing firms from developing countries is far deeper than at first sight appeared to be the case. Competing directly with global giants therefore requires not only similar levels of competences within the firm, but also well-orchestrated collaboration with a highly capable global value chain. Further, while the increasing dominance and capabilities of systems integrators make *competing against* these leading firms extraordinarily challenging, the cascade effect substantially raises the standard of *working for* systems integrators at a global level. The requirements for entry into high value-added parts of global value chains, in terms of R&D, financing, and management skills, have risen substantially for firms in developing countries. For example, in order to work for Boeing as a direct aerospace supplier, one must compete with GE, Rolls-Royce and Pratt & Whitney in aero engines, Vought and Alenia in aero-structures, Rockwell Collins and Honeywell in avionics, and the likes of Bridgestone, Goodyear, Michelin, Saint-Gobain, Alcoa and Alcan in key components and materials. Each of these suppliers also benefits from economies of scale and scope in a similar set of value chain activities. In these three cases, the outcome of the global business revolution seems to point to the exclusion of firms in low-income countries from higher value-added activities in global value chains.

Value chain researchers have sometimes pointed to the possibility for firms in developing countries to upgrade their capabilities by participating in the value chains of global giants, starting as low-end suppliers rather than competitors. Kaplinsky and Morris (2000) described a path of integrating into the global economy involving continued upgrading of the capabilities of local firms: from implementing better processes, to producing better products and services, to performing more valuable functions in the value chain, and eventually to participating in a higher value-added value chain. Each succession of value chain positions involved higher value-added from increased capabilities of the local firms. This optimistic path for firms in developing countries seems to be easier said than done, for each upgrade involves intense battles against entrenched rivals who have become increasingly dominant in high value-added segments of the value chain due to the cascade effect.

To evaluate the possibilities of 'upgrading' in the value chains orchestrated by powerful MNCs, one must have a deep understanding of global value chain dynamics and the relationships between MNCs from high-income countries and firms from low-income countries. Different views have been proposed with regards to the relationship between MNCs and the development of local industries. In its studies on MNCs, the United Nations Conference on Trade and Development (UNCTAD) has consistently adopted the view that when entering local markets of low-income countries, MNCs can establish important 'backward linkages' through local supplier relationships that transmit knowledge and skills to indigenous firms. It further argues that a dense network of such linkages can 'promote production efficiency, productivity growth, technological and managerial capabilities and market diversification for the firms involved' (UNCTAD, 2001: xxi). Spillovers from these linkages can then contribute to a vibrant enterprise sector in low-income countries.

At the same time, there are other views that regard the multinational corporation as an imperialist instrument blocking the economic development of low-income countries. Lenin (1917) argued that the massive capital exports from capitalist countries to low-income countries were the result of 'overripe' conditions in high-income countries, where capital could no longer find profitable investments in an industry environment dominated by monopolistic firms. Instead of raising the living standards of the impoverished masses in the home country, capital was exported to 'backward countries,' where 'capital is scarce, the price of land is relatively low, wages are low, [and] raw materials are cheap' (ibid.: 77). The export of capital gave rise to 'rentier states' controlled by the class of 'bond holders' (rentiers), who 'take no part in production [and] whose profession is idleness' (ibid.: 78). Instead of re-investing in the industrial development of backward countries, monopolistic profits generated by capital exports were promptly extracted and returned to the home country in order to 'bribe its lower classes into acquiescence' (ibid.: 121).

Similarly, Hymer (1976) proposed that one of the key reasons for firms to establish foreign operations was to form collusive networks and eliminate competition. Unlike Marshall (1920), who believed that capitalist firms would rise and fall like trees in a forest, Hymer believed that the capitalist firm is capable of growing in size until it completely dominates entire industries. He observed that as capitalist firms grew large, they acquired ever-more complex administrative structures to coordinate their activities and 'a larger brain to plan for their survival and growth' (Hymer, 1979: 54). Like Lenin, Hymer saw the multinational corporation as an obstacle for low-income countries to attain economic development and social transformation. In his analysis, the multinational firms would eventually dominate the political process of low-income countries they invest in due to the great disparity in bargaining powers. They would then use both their economic and political powers to turn low-income countries into 'branch-plant' countries in both political and economic terms:

> A regime of North Atlantic Multinational Corporations would tend to produce a hierarchical division of labour between geographical regions corresponding to the vertical division of labour within the firm. It would tend to centralize high-level decision-making occupations in a few key cities in the advanced countries, surrounded by a number of regional sub-capitals, and confine the rest of the world to lower levels of activity and income, that is, to the status of towns and villages in a New Imperial System. Income, status, authority and consumption patterns would radiate out from these centres along a declining curve and the existing pattern of inequality and dependency would be perpetuated. (Hymer, 1979: 55)

Instead of an agent for economic development, MNCs are viewed as a 'vast suction pump' for monopoly capitalism to obtain resources from the periphery (Jenkins, 1984: 29).

Our preliminary study of aerospace, beverage, and retail value chains in China has found that in all cases, MNCs have formed local linkages to undertake locally coordinated activities. Many of these local relationships have transcended the simple price relationship. For local firms that have successfully entered the local value chains of MNCs, many of them have been able to upgrade their capabilities through the support of MNCs in a wide range of areas including management, technical know-how, human resources, financing and branding. The increased capabilities have projected the local firms onto an elevated path of higher revenue and/or profit growth. However, continued profitable growth is not guaranteed for local firms in the MNC value chain. In all cases, MNCs have no interest in seeing the emergence of powerful local suppliers that could threaten to hold up system profits. When one or a group of successful supplier(s) grows too powerful, new suppliers or partners are introduced to balance the power of existing ones and dissipate the rent originally allocated. The MNC is therefore not always a benevolent 'nurturer' of local businesses capabilities. Its actions always follow revenues and profits rather than the specific goal of developing local industries. In all three value chains, most of the highest value-added segments are dominated by the systems integrators' highly capable multinational partners headquartered in high-income countries.

6.2.3   At the periphery

Throughout the twentieth century, large capitalist firms stood at the centre of technological progress and economic growth in high-income countries (Chandler, Amatori and Hikino, 1997). One may argue that this was the underlying view that guided the so-called 'East Asian model' of economic development, in which latecoming countries such as Japan and South Korea developed powerful capitalist firms through state-guided industrial policy in the second half of the twentieth century. Given the formidable difficulties of catch-up in the global business revolution, the cost of building national champions that can compete on the global playing field seems to have escalated for developing countries. In fact, in the era of the global business revolution, one may even question whether it is at all possible for developing countries to build new powerful firms that can compete with the existing giants that are dominating nearly all aspects of our economic life. At the same time, policy makers in developing countries often face many other economic, social and political priorities that compete for resources with the goal of building national champions. This situation makes the free-market argument even more tempting for policy makers: simply let the market allocate economic resources with minimal state intervention.

Liberalists argue that the role of the government in the economy should be limited to the provision of public goods, the remedy of market failures, and a certain degree of social security to maintain social stability: 'the role of the government is to be a humble and honest servant [to the market]' (Wolf, 2005: 76). In this view, industrial policy is generally misguided and ineffective, especially in developing countries, where governments are generally 'incompetent, corrupt, or both' and are therefore incapable of devising and executing sound economic policy (ibid.: 73). While the argument against industrial policy has not been supported by historical evidence,[65] it is becoming increasingly difficult for developing countries to build national champions in today's global business environment, which is dominated by powerful MNCs from high-income countries. In order to challenge the formidable competitive advantages of these MNCs, developing countries must invest an enormous amount of resources that could be instead spent on education, healthcare, and social security.

Here the uncomfortable implication for developing countries is that if their policy makers let the process of globalization freely run its course, the 'commanding heights' of their economies, which include the systems integration and other high value-added functions in the value chain, will likely be controlled by powerful multinational firms headquartered in high-income countries. Their economies will have to depend on foreign firms for core technology, key products and services, as well as access to global markets.

The economic dependence of firms from low-income countries on MNCs is highly pronounced in the global retail industry. As a critical part of their strategy to lower cost, large retailers from high-income countries have set up global procurement operations constantly seeking lower cost sources. In doing so, they have become an important agent in global commodity trade and a critical link between consumers in high-income countries and firms in developing countries. For example, Wal-Mart sourced US$ 15 billion-worth of commodity products from China in 2003. If the retailer were a country, it would have been China's fifth largest importer that year, behind Germany but ahead of the United Kingdom, France, Italy, Australia and Russia (see Table 6.6).

Because of the global retailers' massive purchasing power, they have become key customers for a large number of businesses in developing countries. For example, Wal-Mart controlled the world's largest clothing budget, estimated at US$ 35 billion in 2000. In 2002, the retailer bought 14 per cent of the US$ 1.9 billion in apparel that Bangladesh shipped to the United States.[66] The Wal-Mart business has become vital to the economic stability of many small low-income countries, such as Bangladesh and Honduras, some of which regularly send high-level

Table 6.6   China's top ten importers in 2003[a]

Rank	Country	Total imports (US$ billion)
1	USA	92.5
2	Japan	59.4
3	Korea	20.1
4	Germany	17.5
5	Wal-Mart	15.0
6	UK	10.8
7	France	7.2
8	Italy	6.7
9	Australia	6.3
10	Russia	6.0

Source: compiled by author from Ministry of Commerce statistics and company interviews.
Note: [a] Excluding Hong Kong and Taiwan.

government envoys to Bentonville, Arkansas.[67] In addition, many global retailers have also expanded store operations in developing countries (emerging markets) and have significantly affected the structure of indigenous retail industries. Through sourcing and store operations, these global retailers are exerting a significant impact on industry structure, labour standards and consumer welfare in these countries.

The economic dependence on a few multinational firms brings inherent instability and volatility. The low value-added positions of the firms from developing countries in global value chains are usually associated with low switching costs. While MNCs can move from one supplier to another, and from one country to another, with relative ease, developing countries often find it hard to replace the jobs and the income associated with the work. At the same time, MNCs have been using their bargaining power and global procurement muscle to extract the lowest possible price from their suppliers in low-income countries. For example, for a pair of pants that sells for US$ 38 in the retail stores in the United States, the factory in China is paid only US$ 3, or less than 8 per cent of the total value, for cutting and sewing the pants together (Mager, 2003). Meanwhile, MNC buyers continually search the globe for still-cheaper sources of supply. 'The competition', according to the *Los Angeles Times*, 'pits vendor against vendor, country against country'.[68]

As firms from low-income countries are excluded from higher value-added segments of global value chains, the global business system tends to perpetuate inequality between high- and low-income countries. Statistics show that a majority of the benefits of globalization has so far been limited to a small portion of the world's inhabitants. At the end of the twentieth century, the top fifth of the world's people in the richest countries enjoyed 82 per cent of the expanding export trade and 68 per cent of foreign direct investment – the bottom fifth, barely more than one per cent (UNDP, 1999: 31). Between 1994 and 1998, the net worth of the world's 200 richest people increased from US$ 440 billion to more than US$ 1 trillion (ibid.: 37).

During the process of global economic integration, a small club of global elite, dominated by wealthy individuals and leaders of large global firms, has emerged to control a predominant amount of the world's economic resources (Mazlish and Morss, 2005).

At the same time, a large number of the world's inhabitants continue to live in extreme poverty. As UNDP (1999) points out, more than one quarter of the 4.5 billion people in developing countries still do not have some of life's most basic choices – survival beyond age 40, access to knowledge and minimum private and public services (ibid.: 28). Three billion of them, or one half of the world's population, live on an income of under two dollars a day; an equal number of people have no access to sanitation and two billion have no access to electricity.[69] Nearly 1.3 billion people do not have access to clean water and about 840 million are malnourished (ibid.: 28). At the end of the twentieth century, the assets of the three richest people were more than the combined GNP of the 48 least-developed countries (ibid.: 37).

To conclude, not only do firms from developing countries face immense difficulties in catching up with the leading systems integrators, the visible part of the 'iceberg', but they also face immense difficulties in catching up with the powerful firms that now dominate almost every segment of the supply chain, the invisible part of the 'iceberg' that lies hidden from view beneath the water. However, if firms from developing countries do not catch-up or upgrade in their respective value chains, these countries will have to continue to cope with economic dependence and instability, and most likely, persistent poverty and inequality. At the dawn of the twenty-first century, the reality of the intense industrial concentration among both systems integrators and their entire supply chain, brought about through pressure from the 'cascade effect', presents a comprehensive challenge for both firms and policy makers in developing countries.

Bibliography

Agarwal, A., J. F. Jaffe and G. N. Mandelker, 'The Post-Merger Performance of Acquiring Firms: a Re-examination of an Anomaly', *Journal of Finance*, 47: 4, (September 1992), 1605–21.

Air Liquide, *Annual Report, 2003* (2004).

Amcor Investment Prospectus (May 2002).

Amcor, *Annual Report, 2004* (2005).

Amsden, A. H., *Asia's Next Giant: South Korea and Late Industrialisation* (Oxford: Oxford University Press, 1992).

Anderson, S. and J. Cavanagh, *Top 200: The Rise of Corporate Global Power* (Institute for Policy Studies, 2000).

AT Kearney, 2003 MRO Survey (2003).

Ball Corporation, Ball Presentation at Crédit Suisse First Boston Global Basics Conference (March 2004).

Billings Gazette (29 January 2005).

BOC, *Annual Report, 2003* (2004).

Bonacich, E., L. Cheng, N. Chinchilla, N. Hamilton and P. Ong (eds), *Global Production: The Apparel Industry in the Pacific Rim* (Philadelphia, PA: Temple University Press, 1994).

Boston Consulting Group, *Growing through acquisitions* (Boston: BCG Publishing, 2004).

Bradley, S. and P. Ghemawat, *Wal-Mart Stores, Inc.*, (Cambridge, Mass.: Harvard Business School Publishing, 2002).

Business Week (various dates).

Casson, M. C., 'Transaction costs and the Theory of the Multinational Enterprise', in Rugman, A. (eds), *New Theories of the Multinational Enterprise* (London: Croom Helm, 1982), 24–43.

Castells, M., *The rise of the network society*, 2nd edn (Oxford: Blackwell, 2000).

Chandler, A., *Scale and Scope: the Dynamics of Industrial Capitalism* (Cambridge, MA: Harvard University Press, 1990).

Chandler, A., and T. Hikino, 'The large industrial enterprise and the dynamics of modern economic growth', in Chandler *et al.* (eds), *Big Business and the Wealth of Nations* (Cambridge: Cambridge University Press, 1997).

Chandler, A., F. Amatori and T. Hikino (eds), *Big Business and the Wealth of Nations* (Cambridge: Cambridge University Press, 1997).

Chandler Jr, A. and B. Mazlish (eds), *Leviathans: Multinational Corporations and the New Global History* (Cambridge: Cambridge University Press, 2005).

Chang, Ha-Joon, *Kicking Away the Ladder* (London: Anthem Press, 2002).

CNN Money (28 January 2005).

Coase, R. H., *The Firm, the Market, and the Law* (Chicago: University of Chicago Press, 1988).

Coase, R. H., 'The nature of the firm', *Economica*, 4 (1937), 386–405, reprinted in R. H. Coase (1988) (originally published 1937).

Coca-Cola, *Annual Report* (various years).

Constar, *Annual Report, 2003* (2004).

Cotterill, R., 'Dynamic Explanations of Industry Structure and Performance', commissioned paper presented at USDA Conference 'The American Consumer and the Changing Structure of the Food System', Washington DC (3–5 May 2000).

Crédit Suisse First Boston, *The Emergence of Big Box National Retailers* (26 July 2005).

Crédit Suisse First Boston, *Food Investor's Handbook* (August 2005).

Crédit Suisse First Boston, *The New Brand Matrix: exclusive national brands join good, better, best* (23 September 2005).

Crédit Suisse First Boston Equity Research (September 2005).

Crown, *Annual Report, 2003* (2004).

Department of Trade and Industry (DTI), *The UK R&D Scoreboard 2003* (Edinburgh: DTI, 2003).

Department of Trade and Industry (DTI), *The UK R&D Scoreboard 2004* (Edinburgh: DTI, 2004).

Dicken, P., *Global Shift* (Thousand Oaks: Sage Publications, 2003).

Dolan, K. C. and J. Humphrey, 'Value Chains and Upgrading: the Impact of UK Retailers on the Fresh Fruit and Vegetable Industries in Africa', *Journal of Development Studies*, 37: 2, (2000), 147–71.

Dosi, G., M. Hobday, L. Marengo and A. Prencipe, 'The Economics of Systems Integration: Towards an Evolutionary Interpretation', in A. Prencipe, A. Davis and M. Hobday (eds), *The Business of Systems Integration* (Oxford: Oxford University Press, 2003), 95–113.

EADS, *Annual Report, 2004* (2005).

Economist (29 January 2001).

Ellis, J. and J. Heinbockel, 'Global Retailing 2000: a statistical and conceptual view' (Goldman Sachs Investment Research, 27 October 1999).

Euromonitor Database.

Euromonitor, 'Aerospace in the USA', (July 2003a).

Financial Times (FT), various issues.

Find/SVP, *Commercial Aircraft Maintenance, Repair and Overhaul (MRO) Industry* (August 2002).

Fortune magazine, various issues.

Friedman, M., *Capitalism and Freedom* (Chicago: University of Chicago Press, 1962).

Gabel, M. and H. Bruner, *Global Inc: An Atlas of the Multinational Corporation* (New York: New Press, 2003).

Gereffi, G., 'International Trade and Industrial Upgrading by Developing Countries in the Global Apparel Commodity Chain', *Journal of Industrial Economics*, 48: 1, (1999), 37–70.

Gereffi, G., J. Humphrey, R. Kaplinsky and T. Sturgeon 'Globalisation, Value Chains and Development', *IDS Bulletin*, 32: 3, (July 2001), 1–8.

Ghemawat, P. *et al.*, *Wal-Mart Stores in 2003* (Cambridge, MA: Harvard Business School Publishing, 2004).

Gholz, E., 'Systems Integration in the US Defence Industry: Who Does It and Why Is It Important?', in A. Prencipe, A. Davis and M. Hobday (eds), *The Business of Systems Integration* (Oxford: Oxford University Press, 2003), 279–306.

Goldman Sachs Investment Research (October 1999).

Goldman Sachs Investment Research (2003).

Gregory, A., 'An Examination of the Long Run Performance of UK Acquiring Firms', *Journal of Business Finance and Accounting*, 24, (1997), 971–1002.

Humphrey, J. and H. Schmitz, 'Governance in Global Value Chains', *IDS Bulletin*, 32: 3, (2001).

Husky. *Annual Report 2002* and *Annual Report 2003* (2003 and 2004 respectively).

Hymer, S., 'The multinational corporation and the law of uneven development' (1972), reprinted in H. Radice (ed.), *International Firms and Modern Imperialism* (Harmondsworth: Penguin, 1975).

Hymer, S., *The International Operations of National Firms: A Study of Direct Foreign Investment* (Cambridge, MA: MIT Press, 1976).

Hymer, S., *The Multinational Corporation, A Radical Approach: Papers by Stephen Herbert Hymer* (Cambridge: Cambridge University Press, 1979).

IC Insights, http://www.icinsight.com

IHT (International Herald Tribune), 8 July 1999.

Interpublic, *Annual Report, 2004* (2005).

International Institute for Strategic Studies (IISS), *Military Balance, 1999/2000* (London: IISS, 1999).

International Mass Retail Association, *Statement of the International Mass Retail Association Before the Committee on Ways and Means of the US House of Representatives on US-China Economic Relations and China's Role in the Global Economy* (31 October 2003).

James, A. D., *Post-merger Strategies of the Leading US Defence Aerospace Companies* (Stockholm: Defence Research Establishment, FOA-R-98-00941-170-SE, 1998).

Jenkins, R., *Transnational Corporations and Industrial Transformation in Latin America* (London: Macmillan, 1984).

Johnson, C., *Miti and the Japanese Miracle: The Growth of Industrial Policy 1925–1975* (Stanford: Stanford University Press, 1983).

Kaplinsky, R. and M. Morris, *Handbook for Value Chain Research* (Cambridge: Institute of Development Studies, 2000), at <http://www.ids.ac.uk/ids/global/pdfs/VchNov01.pdf>.

KHS, *Annual Report, 2003* (2004).

Krones, *Annual Report, 2003* (2004).

Lehman Brothers, *The Global Water Industry* (29 January 2002).

Lenin, V. I., *Imperialism, the Highest Stage of Capitalism* (London: Lawrence & Wishart, 1917).

Linde, *Annual Report, 2003* (2004).

Mager, M., *The Essentials of Apparel: Wholesale and Retail* (Goldman Sachs Global Equity Research, 27 August 2003).

Malone, T. W. and R. L. Laubacher, 'The Dawn of the E-Lance Economy', *Harvard Business Review* (September–October 1998).

Marshall, A., *Principles of Economics* (London: Macmillan, 1920, 1st edn 1890).

Marx, K., *Capital, Vol. 1* (1867) (New York: International Publishers, 1967 edn).

Mazlish, B. and E. R. Morss, 'A Global Elite?', in A. Chandler Jr and B. Mazlish (eds), *Leviathans: Multinational Corporations and the New Global History* (Cambridge: Cambridge University Press, 2005), 167–86.

Meeks, G., *Disappointing marriage* (Cambridge: Cambridge University Press, 1977).

Merrill Lynch, *Blueprint for Media Investment* (London: Merrill Lynch, 2002).

Morgan Stanley, *The Competitive Edge* (New York and London: MSDW, 1998).

Morgan Stanley, *The Competitive Edge* (New York and London: MSDW, 1999).

Morgan Stanley, *Annual Report, 2004* (2005).

Murman, E. *et al.*, *Lean Enterprise Value: Insights from MIT's Lean Aerospace Initiative* (New York: Palgrave Macmillan, 2002).

Nolan, P., *China's Rise, Russia's Fall: Politics, Economics and Planning in the Transition from Stalinism* (London: Palgrave Macmillan, 1995).

Nolan, P., *Indigenous Large Firms in China's Economic Reform* (London: Contemporary China Institute, School of Oriental and African Studies, University of London, 1998).

Nolan, P., *Coca-Cola and the Global Business Revolution: A Study with Special Reference to the EU* (Cambridge: Judge Institute of Management Studies, 1999).

Nolan, P., *China and the Global Business Revolution* (London: Palgrave Macmillan, 2001a)

Nolan, P., *China and the Global Economy* (London: Palgrave Macmillan, 2001b)

Nolan, P. and H. Rui, 'Industrial policy and the global big business revolution: the case of the Chinese coal industry', *Journal of Chinese Economic and Business Studies*, 2:2 (May, 2004a), 97–113.

Nolan, P. and H. Rui, *The cascade effect and the Chinese steel industry* (mimeo, 2004b).

Nolan, P. and J. Zhang, *Industrial Consolidation, the Cascade Effect and the Challenges of the Global Business Revolution for Developing Countries: the Case of Aerospace and Beverages*, paper prepared for Conference on International Competitiveness of China's Industries, Ministry of Commerce, China, Xiamen (September 2004).

Omnicom, *Annual Report, 2004* (2005).

Owens-Illinois, *Annual Report, 2003* (2004).

Paarlberg, P. and M. Haley, 'Market Concentration and Vertical Coordination in the Pork Industry: Implications for Public Policy Analysis', paper presented at USDA Conference 'The American Consumer and the Changing Structure of the Food System', Washington, DC, 3–5 May 2000.

Paoli, M., 'The Cognitive Basis of Systems Integration: Redundancy of Context-generating Knowledge', in A. Prencipe, A. Davis and M. Hobday (eds), *The Business of Systems Integration* (Oxford: Oxford University Press, 2003), 152–73.

Penrose, E., *The Theory of the Growth of the Firm* (Oxford: Oxford University Press, 1995, 2nd edn).

PepsiCo, *Annual Report, 2004* (2005).

Piore, M. and C. Sabel, *The Second Industrial Divide: Possibilities for Progress* (New York: Basic Books, 1984).

Plastipak, *Annual Report, 2003* (2004).

Porter, M., *The Competitive Advantage of Nations* (London: Macmillan, 1990).

Prais, S. J., *Productivity and Industrial Structure* (Cambridge: Cambridge University Press, 1981).

Pratten, C., *Economies of Scale in Manufacturing Industry* (Cambridge: Cambridge University Press, 1971).

Praxair, *Annual Report, 2003* (2004).

Prencipe, A., 'Corporate Strategy and Systems Integration Capabilities: Managing Networks in Complex Systems Industries', in A. Prencipe, A. Davis and

M. Hobday (eds), *The Business of Systems Integration* (Oxford: Oxford University Press, 2003), 114–33.

Radice, H. (ed.), *International Firms and Modern Imperialism* (Harmondsworth: Penguin, 1975).

Ravenscraft, D. J. and F. M. Scherer, *Mergers, Sell-offs and Economic Efficiency* (Washington, DC: Brookings Institution, 1987).

Rexam, *Annual Report* (various years).

Rexam, *Global Packaging Trends, Facts and Insight*, Consumer Packaging Report (2003).

Rexam, US Investor Roadshow Presentation (March 2003).

Richardson, G., 'The Organisation of Industry', *Economic Journal*, 82 (1972), 883–96.

Roach, B. 'A Primer on Multinational Corporations' in A. Chandler, Jr. and B. Mazlish (eds), *Leviathans: Multinational Corporations and the New Global History* (Cambridge: Cambridge University Press, 2005), 19–44.

Rogers, R., 'Structural Change in US Food Manufacturing, 1958 to 1997', paper presented at USDA Conference 'The American Consumer and the Changing Structure of the Food System', Washington, DC, 3–5 May 2000.

Rugman, A., 'Internalisation and Non-equity Forms of Internal Involvement', in A. Rugman (eds), *New Theories of the Multinational Enterprise* (London: Croom Helm, 1982), 9–23.

Ruigrok, W. and R. van Tulder, *The Logic of International Restructuring* (London: Routledge, 1995).

Saint-Gobain, *Annual Report, 2004* (2005).

Sapolsky, H. M., 'Inventing Systems Integration', in A. Prencipe, A. Davis and M. Hobday (eds), *The Business of Systems Integration* (Oxford: Oxford University Press, 2003), 15–34.

Schmitz, H. and P. Knorringa, 'Learning From Global Buyers' in *Journal of Development Studies*, 32:7, (2000), 177–205.

SCMP (South China Morning Post), 29 March 2004.

Sidel, *Annual Report, 1998* (1999).

Simpson, J. and D. Gavin, *The Boeing 767: From Concept to Production* (Cambridge, MA: Harvard Business School Publishing, 1991).

SIPRI, Military Expenditure and Arms Production Project (June 2003).

Sorrell, M., 'The advertising and marketing services industry: outlook good and getting better', in WPP, *Annual Report, 2004* (WPP, 2005).

Steinmueller, E. W., 'The Role of Technical Standards in Coordinating the Division of Labour in Complex System Industries', in A. Prencipe, A. Davis and M. Hobday (eds), *The Business of Systems Integration* (Oxford: Oxford University Press, 2003), 133–51.

Technology Review (December 2004).

Tetra Laval, *Annual Report, 2004* (2005).

ThyssenKrupp, *Annual Report 2001–2002* (2003).

UNCTAD, *World Investment Report 2000: Cross-border Mergers and Acquisitions and Development* (Geneva: UN Publications, 2000).

UNCTAD, *World Investment Report 2001: Promoting Linkages* (Geneva: UN Publications, 2001).

UNCTAD, *World Investment Report 2002: Multinational Corporations and Export Competitiveness* (Geneva: UN Publications, 2002).

UNDP, *Human Development Report 1999: Globalization with a Human Face* (New York and Oxford: Oxford University Press, 1999).

Volvo, *Annual Report, 2005* (2006).

Wal-Mart, *Annual Report, 2003* (2004).

Walton, S., *Sam Walton: Made in America* (New York: Bantam Books, 1993).

Ward's Auto World, various issues.

Williamson, O. E., 'The Modern Corporation: Origins, Evolution, Attributes', in *Journal of Economic Literature*, 19, (December 1981), 1537–68.

Wolf, M., *Why Globalization Works: The Case for the Global Market Economy* (New Haven: Yale University Press, 2005).

World Bank, *World Development Report, 1998* (New York: Oxford University Press, 1998).

World Bank, *World Development Report, 2002* (New York: Oxford University Press, 2002).

WPP, *Annual Report, 2004* (2005).

Yoffie, D., *Cola Wars Continue: Coke and Pepsi in the Twenty-First Century* (Cambridge, MA: Harvard Business School Publishing, 2004).

Zhen, X., 'To Dismiss the Extensive Growing Model and Follow the Road of New Industrialisation', in Liu Guoguang *et al.* (eds), *Analysis and Forecast on China's Economy 2005* (Beijing: Social Sciences Academic Press, 2004).

Notes

1. Meeks (1977) is the classic study of this topic. The view that 'most mergers fail' is parroted remorselessly among mainstream academics of all ideological persuasions.
2. Friedman neglects to point out that the 'widening of markets' in the nineteenth century was followed by the construction of the monster firm, US Steel. It was formed out of a succession of mergers, culminating in the merger in 1900 of Carnegie Steel and Federal Steel. US Steel then accounted for 60–70 per cent of all major steel products sold in the United States (Nolan, 2001a: 601).
3. A more 'methodologically correct' way is to compare country GDPs with the value-added of corporations. Using this method, 37 of the 100 largest economies in the world in 1999 would have been corporations (Wolf, 2005).
4. Aggregate cross-border M&A data in this chapter are obtained from UNCTAD (2000), and aggregate US M&A data are obtained from SDC runs, unless otherwise specified.
5. UNCTAD's figures in fact understate the importance of horizontal M&As, because many of the conglomerate transactions involve a subsidiary of a conglomerate merging or acquiring a competitor in the same industry.
6. Driven by one large deal, namely the US$ 165 billion merger between AOL and Time Warner.
7. In fact, these data understate the true degree of concentration, because many firms focus on specific sub-branches of their sector. For example, within the pharmaceutical industry, in many therapies, just one or two firms account for almost the entire global market.
8. Airlines remain one of the exceptions to the rule of industrial consolidation. Most industry experts believe that if national restrictions on airline consolidation were removed, there would be just a handful of giant airlines that would dominate global markets.
9. Tupolev alone produced almost 2,000 Tu-134s and Tu-154s, which placed it roughly on a par with McDonnell Douglas, though far short of Boeing.
10. Mike Sears, 'The Bottom Line on Lean: A CFO's Perspective', speech given on the Lean Aerospace Initiative, 10 April 2001.
11. Ibid.
12. Boeing also invites each supplier that is evaluated to provide a satisfaction rating for Boeing itself through an anonymous online report. The results of the evaluation are provided to Boeing's senior management.
13. The most immediate, visible manifestation of this journey is the newly established assembly line for the 737 in Seattle, which is in continuous motion as subsystems are added to the fuselage. Each plane on the line moves at two inches per hour, and takes seven to eight days to assemble. Boeing is in the process of reducing the number of 'touch hours' it takes to assemble, from over 5,000 to around 4,000.
14. Compared with 15 divestitures in the same period.

15. Quoted in *The True Cost of Subcontracting Work to Low-Cost Economies*, by Bravura Consulting Ltd, March 2004.
16. It is Composite Technology Research Malaysia (CTRM).
17. The same applies to wine and spirits, but these will not be analysed in this book.
18. In 2003, US$ 732 billion was spent globally on 'specialist communications'.
19. In 2002, the world's top ten spenders on advertising, all firms headquartered in the high-income countries, spent an average of US$ 2.5 billion each on advertising (Sorrell, 2005).
20. Yoffie (2004).
21. According to Coca-Cola executives, CCE accounted for one-fifth of Coca-Cola's global beverage sales in 2003. Coca-Cola's total global sales are therefore calculated by multiplying CCE's sales by five.
22. This is partly because Coca-Cola built many of its overseas bottling plants along with the movements of American troops during and after the Second World War in order to supply the US military.
23. 'Brands in an Age of Anti-Americanism', *Business Week*, 4 August 2003.
24. A rough estimate based on the fact that Greater Europe accounted for around 29 per cent of Coca-Cola's total net sales in 1997. A study of Coca-Cola in Europe showed that within the EU alone in 1997, the Coca-Cola system (including the bottling companies) spent over US$ 7 billion on its major purchases of goods and services (Nolan, 1998). This included around over US$ 1.4 billion on packaging, around US$ 1 billion on ingredients, US$ 800 million on distribution, US$ 440 million on marketing equipment, US$ 350 million on new plant and production line equipment, and over US$ 100 million on utilities.
25. The price of concentrate is at the heart of the relationship between the company and the bottlers. The Coca-Cola Company has to balance the short-term incentive to drive up the price of concentrate against the long-term incentive for the bottlers to reinvest, grow and remain committed to building the Coca-Cola business.
26. The term 'anchor bottler' is no longer used by Coca-Cola.
27. Substantial technical developments were necessary to allow production of the contour can. However, the contour can has still not been widely used in beverages.
28. Today glass is still the main form of primary packaging in the beer industry.
29. Saint-Gobain claims to produce 30 billion bottles annually (Saint-Gobain, *Annual Report, 2004*), so we may safely assume that together, the two companies produce more than 60 billion glass bottles each year.
30. Even today, almost two decades after privatization, there is a 'hard core' of leading French entities that control almost one-fifth of the company's voting shares. These include the Saint-Gobain Savings Plan, the Caisses des Dépôts et Consignations, BNP Paribas, and AXA. The board of directors contains representatives of many of France's leading companies. These include Daniel Bernard, CEO of Carrefour, Gerard Mertraller, CEO of Suez, Michel Pebereu, Chairman of BNP Paribas, and Dennis Ranques, CEO of Thales.
31. This important aspect of technical progress in the industry will not be dealt with in this book.

32. These technologies constitute a barrier against the penetration of oxygen and the leakage of carbon dioxide respectively.
33. SEN and AG Holstein each has a venerable history in the German machine-building industry. Holstein & Kappert (H&K) was founded in 1868. SEN was formed from a three-way merger in 1982, between Seitz-Werke, which was founded in 1887, L.A. Enzinger, which was founded in 1878 and Noll. Unlike H&K or SEN, Klöckner-Werke has been involved in a variety of industrial activities after its inception in 1923. Only in the 1980s and the 1990s, did Klöckner start to focus on the packaging industry, and gradually pull out of other activities such as automotive supply. Already, in 1979 it purchased a 51 per cent shareholding in H&K and in 1982 it acquired a 24 per cent share of SEN Corporation. This paved the way for the final merger in 1993.
34. 'The middle of the road is clearly becoming an increasingly difficult place to be, with traffic coming from both directions. Those agencies excluded from the super-agency pitches because they lack the scale and resources must now be feeling distinctly uncomfortable. Our business is increasingly polarizing between the very big at one end and the small at the other' (Sorrell, 2005).
35. General Motors, Microsoft, Johnson & Johnson, Nestlé and Unilever.
36. 'The bigger the media buying operation, the more clout it wields in negotiating the cheapest rates from the media owner, giving it a boost in the competition for clients' (Sorrell, 2005).
37. Source: US Bureau of Labor Statistics.
38. Source: Ellis and Heinbockel (1999).
39. Calculated by author from Mager (2003).
40. Source: Ellis and Heinbockel (1999).
41. Source: Company website.
42. Source: Ghemawat *et al.* (2004).
43. Ibid.
44. Wal-Mart, *Annual Report, 2003*: 2.
45. Ibid.
46. 'The First Trillion-Dollar Company', Lisa DiCarlo, *Forbes*.com, 2003.
47. 'One Nation Under Wal-Mart', Jerry Useem, *Fortune*, 3 March 2003.
48. Source: Ellis and Heinbockel (1999).
49. Ibid.
50. Source: Ghemawat *et al.* (2004: 6).
51. Source: Ghemawat *et al.* (2004).
52. Source: Bradley and Ghemawat (2002: 6).
53. Information on Retail Link is obtained from Ghemawat *et al.* (2004).
54. 'How the Competition Can Stay Profitable in the Shadow of a Giant', Neil Buckly, *Financial Times*, 8 July 2004.
55. Source: Ghemawat *et al.* (2004).
56. Walton (1993: 238).
57. Ghemawat *et al.* (2004).
58. Data obtained from CSFB equity research report, *The Food Industry Handbook* (August 2005), excludes Wal-Mart sales.
59. For a more detailed discussion on the pork and swine growing industries, see Paarlberg and Haley (2000).

60. According to the NDP Group, the US$ 135 billion US apparel market is segmented into 'Designer' (US$ 3 billion), 'Bridge' (US$ 4 billion), 'Better' (US$ 34 billion), 'Moderate' (US$ 51 billion), and 'Mass' (US$ 44 billion) markets.

61. For example, BP is not only one of the world's leading petrochemical producers, but also it alone accounts for around two-fifths of the world's total PTA production. GSK not only is one of the world's top pharmaceutical companies, but also within the therapies for anti-asthma and anti-herpes drugs, it accounts for around one-third and almost one-half respectively of total global sales. Samsung, Hynix, Micron, Infineon and Toshiba are all leading semiconductor producers, but in the market for NANDflash memory chips, Samsung, Toshiba and Hynix together account for around nine-tenths of the world total, and in the market for DRAMS, Samsung, Micron, Infineon and Hynix together account for around three-quarters of the world total. Within the telecommunications equipment market, Nokia accounts for over one-third of the total world market for mobile phones, while Cisco accounts for over two-thirds of the total global market for routers. Not only is Microsoft one of the world's leading software companies, but also in the market for PC operating systems it accounts for over 80 per cent of the total global market, while IBM, Microsoft and Oracle between them account for around nine-tenths of the total global market for database software.

62. In 2003, just four of the top 700 firms by R&D expenditure were from low- and middle-income countries, two from China and two from Brazil. There were nine firms from Korea and seven from Taiwan (DTI, 2004).

63. Economists' reduction of 'technical progress' to the so-called 'residual' in the 'production function', which remains after account has been taken of the contribution to economic growth of increased inputs of 'capital' and 'labour', is embarrassingly superficial.

64. Indeed, the common response of most economists, both 'radical' and mainstream, is denial, and endless manipulation of data to attempt to 'prove' that industrial concentration is not in fact taking place, and to suggest that technical progress, insofar as it is acknowledged to be taking place, is the product mainly of small and medium-sized firms. However, the reality of the technical transformation of this epoch and the consequences of oligopolistic competition for real price declines, are obvious to most people through their daily lives.

65. Through different measures of industrial policy, a succession of latecomer countries have successfully cultivated powerful indigenous firms that proved instrumental to the economic catch-up of these countries. These included Great Britain during the Industrial Revolution, the United States and Continental Europe in the nineteenth century, Japan, the Republic of Korea, and Singapore in the second half of the twentieth century (see Johnson, 1983; Amsden, 1992; Nolan, 1995; Chang, 2002; Nolan and Zhang, 2004). Without the continuous collective support from the most powerful governments in Europe, Airbus probably would never succeeded in challenging Boeing's leadership in aerospace. The profile of Boeing today resulted from industrial policy exercised by the US Department of Defense, which has orchestrated the consolidation in the American defence and aerospace industry at the end of the 1990s.

66. Nancy Cleeland, Evelyn Iritani and Tyler Marshall, 'Scouring the Globe to Give Shoppers an US$ 8.63 Polo Shirt', *LA Times*, 24 November 2003.
67. Ibid.
68. Ibid.
69. Source: World Resources Institute, at <www.wri.org>.

Index

Note: 'n.' after a page reference indicates the number of a note on that page.